SOUTH ESSEX

Edited by Michelle Warrington

First published in Great Britain in 1999 by
POETRY NOW YOUNG WRITERS
Remus House, Coltsfoot Drive,
Woodston,
Peterborough, PE2 9JX
Telephone (01733) 890066

HB ISBN 0 75430 439 6
SB ISBN 0 75430 440 X

FOREWORD

This year, the Poetry Now Young Writers'
Kaleidoscope competition proudly presents the best
poetic contributions from over 32,000 up-and-coming
writers nationwide.

Successful in continuing our aim of promoting
writing and creativity in children, each regional
anthology displays the inventive and original writing
talents of 11-18 year old poets. Imaginative,
thoughtful, often humorous, *Kaleidoscope South
Essex* provides a captivating insight into the issues
and opinions important to today's young generation.

The task of editing inevitably proved challenging, but
was nevertheless enjoyable thanks to the quality of
entries received. The thought, effort and hard work
put into each poem impressed and inspired us all. We
hope you are as pleased as we are with the final result
and that you continue to enjoy *Kaleidoscope South
Essex* for years to come.

CONTENTS

Hassenbrook School

Robert Clack School

St Clere's GM School

The Poems

THE MAGICAL WINDOW

The beautiful she,
Brought by her mother into the world
Admired and kind-hearted,
She asks her mother if she could play outside
Her eyes see sunshine out of the magical window
Which did not show
Her mother suspects rain
She tells her to wait,
But kind-hearted, she refuses to listen,
So she steps outside to play.
At that sudden moment thunder clatters.
'Mother oh Mother! Why didn't I listen?'
She cries, blaming herself.
She rushes back inside
And looks through the magical window
But all she sees is a false sunshine.
The innocent, she never looked through there again.

Gareshma Bheitia (15)

THE SEASIDE

People splashing in the sea
Children running around eating ice-cream
Mothers sunbathing on their lilos
Little boys playing football on the sand
Boys and girls jumping from the pier into the sea
Little girls trying to jump over the waves
People surfing in the deep blue sea
All this happening in front of me.

Nicole Gilligan (12)
Brentwood Ursuline Convent High School

THE SEA

A still sheet of silk
Lay in the night
When the sun rises . . .
There's a radiant light.

Under the water
The whales awake
As the surface of water
Begins to shake.

There are bubbles and splashing
What could this be?
A mermaid I tell you . . .
In front of me.

She waved and splashed
Was she a con?
A wave submerged her . . .
She was gone.

The sun is setting
It's getting cold
The light has gone . . .
The darkness unfolds.

Amy Hooks (12)
Brentwood Ursuline Convent High School

SEAL'S PUPS

S ee that head bobbing up and down!
E very minute it keeps ducking down!
A ll over the shore they sunbathe all day
L istening to the cries of their young seal pups at play.
,
S lipping silently into the water playing with those delightful fish

P ushing and pulling they catch their prey, oh I'm so hungry,
       I could eat a whole dish!
U nder the waves their mothers call them,
P lease can we stay and dance in the sun,
S urely it's sunset, the night has begun.

Michelle Chardin (12)
Brentwood Ursuline Convent High School

DOLPHINS

D olphins, dolphins, splashing high,
O ver the blue waves, under the sky,
L arger than manatee, smaller than whales,
P ushing through the seaweed as it swims so fast,
H igh and deep in the big velvet sea,
I n the white waves as it glides,
N aughty little dolphin splashing around,
S leepy and tired the dolphin sleeps,
       ready to rise in the morning.

Faye Johnson (12)
Brentwood Ursuline Convent High School

A COLD CHRISTMAS

Children playing in the snow,
The whiteness has settled upon our land,
The cold sets in with little red noses,
The Christmas sigh shows on our faces,
People shivering, people sneezing,
People laughing having fun, ♪
Ponds have frozen the ducks have gone.

Christmas is nearer,
The carol singers we hear,
The colour is white,
The feeling peaceful
Now the pond is frozen,
People start shaking.

Christmas Eve,
Emotions are high,
With the festivity we hear children cry,
Dreams of Santa,
The dreams of snow,
Snowmen have been built,
Just to show off to each and every child,
Santa Claus will come tonight,
With lots of presents in his sight,
Trees are bare with just the snow.

Christmas Day is near,
The log fires are blazing,
People sit comfy eating mince pies,
After Christmas has gone the feeling dies,
People are back to their normal daily lives,
The snow has melted,
The feeling has gone,
All we have now are the memories to live from,
Until next year.

Charlotte Wright (14)
Brentwood Ursuline Convent High School

WHAT IS THE SEA?

The sea is a deep, blue, mysterious adventure,
the big waves crashing against the rocks.
The warm refreshing water,
leading a life of its own.

What is the sea?

The sea is a large swimming pool,
home to swimmers and surfers,
home to sharks and crabs,
coral and seaweed.

What is the sea?

The sea belongs to the hot yellow sand,
where children play to their hearts' content.
Where parents laze,
underneath the bright big sun

What is the sea?

Charlotte Perry (13)
Brentwood Ursuline Convent High School

SANDCASTLE

Pile up the sand inside,
Tip it up close your eyes,
Pull it up, wait for a surprise,
Collect some pebbles,
A crisp packet and lolly stick,
Makes a flag tall and thick,
Build a moat with tunnels to the sea,
Sit and wait for the tide,
Running in and out,
Suddenly it comes right in,
Splishing, splashing all around,
Round and round the moat,
Suddenly we have to go,
Running through the sand,
Rushing to the car,
Peering out the window,
Looking all around,
Suddenly I see it,
A flag floating in the sea . . .

Amy Meikle (12)
Brentwood Ursuline Convent High School

SARASOTA BEACH

Crashing waves on a windy day
Seagulls screeching around the bay
Sand as soft as the driven snow
Sailboats drift as far as they can go
Sun-bleached bodies
Deep blue sea
Paradise as far as the eye can see.

Amanda Lamb (12)
Brentwood Ursuline Convent High School

MIDNIGHT BLUE

M idnight blue is so suspicious,
I s it because of the dark sky?
D angerous and sharp
N ever quiet
I t always seems to jump out at you
G iant puffs of air make rough sounds
H orrifying sounds of doors slamming in the wind
T errifying

B lue can be haunting like witches and black cats
L iving nightmares
U nlikely to be true
E ven though everywhere you look there is midnight blue.

Jennifer Brooks (12)
Brentwood Ursuline Convent High School

WHAT IS THE SEA?

What is the sea?
It is a big pool of water beneath me
Waves crash bang on the rocks
Mysterious colours flicker

What is the sea?
A place of mystery
People free, dancing, smiling gleefully
The sun glistening brightly

I wonder what is the sea?

Sarah Conlon (12)
Brentwood Ursuline Convent High School

PINK

The touch of an angel's wing with a harp,
On a cloud, high above, soft and gentle like a
dove.

It's the taste of fluffy candyfloss and honeysuckle
sweets,
It looks like a heart dressed in pink.

As the sun sets, the clouds turn pink,
Pink can sink in the silver sea.

Pink tinges the colour of the sea shells
Love is the colour pink.

Zenobia Waymouth (11)
Brentwood Ursuline Convent High School

DOLPHINS

D is for dolphins, beautiful and calm,
O is for the oldest animal of the sea,
L is for loving and caring animals,
P is for pain that they feel when they are captured
H is for home which they call the sea
I   is for ill which is caused by pollution,
N is for never hurt dolphins,
S is for save the dolphins!

Lucy Scully (12)
Brentwood Ursuline Convent High School

THE WORLD ENDING

Everything dies, so they say,
And that includes the world, one day.
When will it be, tomorrow, next week,
Am I prepared for the end of the world?

Will I get time to say goodbye,
To understand the reason why.
I am to be parted from my family and friends,
It scares me to think that the world will end.

How will it happen, will it be fast
Will there be pain, I would hate to be last.
To witness everyone around me dying or dead,
Knowing so much will remain unsaid.

No more people, nothing to survive
No plants or birds or animals alive.
No more laughter, no cries no sound,
Just a creepy silence all around.

Joanna Kain (13)
Brentwood Ursuline Convent High School

MY DOLPHIN - UNDERWATER LOVE

My dolphin is nice and kind
If I had to go I would never
Leave my dolphin behind
I love and care for my dolphin
My dolphin is my best friend
This is what I call underwater love.

Cassandra Woods (12)
Brentwood Ursuline Convent High School

PURPLE!

My favourite colour is purple,
It makes me think of circles,
When I see it,
I feel happy because I am with it,
I want to start dancing,
As I think of a deer prancing,"
Exotic countries, exotic flowers,
Purple, I could think of you for hours,
Purple is a tangy sweet,
No other colour could ever beat,
Oh yes,

I can feel the juiciness,
Green and blue, red and black,
I could throw them in a big sack,
Purple should never be taken for granted,
As it's the colour which is enchanted.

Lucy Walker (11)
Brentwood Ursuline Convent High School

DANGER

The sea is full of dangers,
The tide is only one,
It's swept away so many,
And nothing could be done.

Lots of people play in the sea,
'Cause they don't know the danger
The tide comes in and . . .
        Help!

Natalie Doggett (12)
Brentwood Ursuline Convent High School

TITANIC

T he sea raged,
I t roared with anger,
T he people screamed in fear
A wful noises, screaming!
N ot a person wasn't screaming,
I nnocent people about to die!
C rash, sink! The Titanic is lost,
      a dream born to die.

Jade Parker (12)
Brentwood Ursuline Convent High School

FISHING

F ishermen trying to catch us,
I n the deep blue sea.
S wimming along with our shiny scales,
H ooks have caught my brothers and sisters,
I hope they don't catch me.
N o! They've captured some of my friends,
G o away, you won't catch me!

Amy Irvine (12)
Brentwood Ursuline Convent High School

SUNSETS

S unsets are so beautiful
U nder the tree you see it fall
N ight is falling and the sun is yawning
S ometimes you see sunsets on the shimmering sea top
E verywhere is fast asleep
T he darkness of the sunset is calming for all.

Lisa Farquhar (12)
Brentwood Ursuline Convent High School

THE SEA

While looking in the Australian sea
It suddenly occurred to me that there
was life beneath me,
I said looking into the sea.

The sea was rough the sea was tough
I'd suddenly had enough.
Then a crab came and bit my leg
so I hit him in the head.
I took it home and put it to bed.
When I awoke the crab was dead.

The next day I went out again
unfortunately in the pouring rain.
But nothing could keep me away from
the deep, blue, mysterious sea.

It looked like butterflies flying,
spying on me.

Jane Thomas (12)
Brentwood Ursuline Convent High School

PURPLE

The colour purple,
'Be peaceful' it whispers.
Mediterranean reefs with purple coral,
Which calmly float up and down.
Purple is cool, and is instant refreshment.
It's light and bright up in the purple clouds,
So soft as you float calmly.
Purple, so minty, so calm as you lie in bed.
So purple, so cooling, resting your sleepy head.

Cheryl Gallacher (11)
Brentwood Ursuline Convent High School

What Blue Means To Me

What does blue mean to you?
To me it means the sea
Calm on a quiet day splashing up at the bay
The soft froth bubbling silently for hours.

Blue is not red nor is it green
It is rather exciting when it is seen.
The exotic fish that swim in the clear blue sea
Colourful and peaceful swimming with me.
The silky sky above me
High, cool and sweet.

Jessica Sheehy (11)
Brentwood Ursuline Convent High School

The Beach

Little children building sandcastles,
And splashing about in the salty water.
The smell of sweet candyfloss,
And hot fresh doughnuts.

Queuing up at the roller-coaster,
Finally we are on, *arrhhh* and it's ended
I think that it's time to go home now
But first let's watch the beautiful sunset
On the beach.

Aneeka Anderson (12)
Brentwood Ursuline Convent High School

SEA POEM

M any animals live in the sea
A nd swim and play together
M any dangers lurk about in the
M ud, sea and sand
A ll things are scared of something
L urking about in the   *n*
S ea

D olphins are playful and hate to be
O n their own they
L ove to chase each other,
P lay tumble turns and
H urt each other
I n the sea but
N one of them know the dangers in the
S ea

W hales are big mammals
H eavy and slow
A nd any animal can
L eave the whale behind
E verything is scared of something in the
S ea.

Isabel Soper (12)
Brentwood Ursuline Convent High School

14

MUSIC

Some say music is the voice of God,
It sings out to each one of us.
It expresses one's feelings and desires,
Some people consider it a must.

There are songs about love,
There are songs about friendship,
There are songs about hatred too.

There are songs about flying,
There are songs about sailing,
Out on the ocean blue.

Some songs are made from dreams
Some songs nobody knew
All songs have a meaning
Some enlighten or comfort you.

So when you're sitting in a room
And there's nothing to do
Just turn on the radio
And you will find that it's true!

Some say singing is good for the mind
It makes you content and happy
It will help you to unwind
Have a listen and see.

One day you'll be bored
And as lonely as can be
Why not sing and sing and sing
Why not sing yourself silly?

Beth Le Gresley (13)
Bromfords School

PARENTS

Parents, they're so mean.
'It's too late, leave a note if you go out,
don't forget your keys.'
This nagging gets on my nerves . . .

    Parents, they're so mean,
    my curfew is half past eight,
    my pocket money is only a pound.
    All they do is moan,
    I just want to pack a suitcase and leave . . .

Parents, they're so mean,
they always say 'I'm only doing it for your benefit.'
They don't understand
they never consider what I might like to do . . .

    Parents, they're so mean,
    they never buy me decent clothes,
    they never cook the meal I want to eat,
    they're always too busy on the phone
    or washing the car . . .

They're nagging has jumped my last nerve
I can't take it any longer.
All it is, is a repetitive droning sound
constantly nagging in my ear, 'Do this, do that
don't forget this'
Parents they're so mean.

Mitchel Clee (13)
Bromfords School

ISLAND POEM

I saw the deep blue sea
Sparkling and swishing around
People's ankles.
I saw the sparkling sun
Swimming in the sea.
The clouds were as white
And as fluffy as marshmallows
I saw some dolphins swimming,
Having fun in the big blue sea.
I saw the biggest brightest palm trees
And there was a big black cave.

Liam Horan (12)
Eastbury Comprehensive School

THE KOLA BIRD

There it flies through the sky
Beak bright as ever
Feathers green and yellow sparkled in the morning sun
The kola bird soars higher than ever
Weary as its shadow passes across the sea
But on the land
Dangerous the mighty hunter spots his kill
And through his sight he pulls the trigger
And the bird scared as ever
Falls down dead as ever.

Michael Hiden (12)
Eastbury Comprehensive School

ISLAND POEM

I looked down on my island and I could see,
The deepest blue sea and the golden sun.
The palm trees were the greenest green
And I could smell a sweet rich smell
Like sweet fresh candyfloss
There was a dark, enormous cave
And the sky was big and beautiful.
The lovely sunshine was as beautiful as can be
And was shining on a school of beautiful dolphins.
The clouds were like big white balls of cotton wool
And looked softer than ever.
My island had a big expensive money tree,
Which had money falling onto the green grass
And blowing into the sea.
After a while the beautiful sun started to go down.

Vikki Morlang (11)
Eastbury Comprehensive School

ISLAND POEM

The glittering golden beach,
The sparkling beautiful sunshine.
The lovely fresh blue sea,
The darkest giant cave.

The silky silver sharks,
Delicious coconuts.
The greatest bluest swimming pool,
And colourful smoothest fishes.

Joanna Gore (11)
Eastbury Comprehensive School

What I See

I stand on the tallest point of the island, the mountain,
I gaze at the glittering blue sea and stare shocked
So beautiful,
The golden sun making everything glisten and shine,
Dolphins screaming here there everywhere,
The fluffy white clouds against the baby blue sky,
Birds singing and flying with joy,
The green grass blowing gently in the breeze,
Now the sun is setting,
Purples, oranges and yellows,
Soon it will be dark and silent,
Animals will crawl away to sleep.

Shahnaz Khalique (12)
Eastbury Comprehensive School

The Fantasy Island

I saw the clouds as smooth and as white as marshmallows,
The palm trees as bright as a strong torch,
I saw the dry mountains, which were as grey as rainy clouds
The sky as blue as the deep blue sparkling ocean.
I saw a treasure chest which was as glittery as the blue ocean.
I saw the golden sun glistening on a dolphin's back.
A sweet which was as giant as Big Ben,
I saw the swimming pool which was big and deep.

Sarah Fellows (12)
Eastbury Comprehensive School

MY FANTASY

I'm in a meadow,
Far, far away,
The sky filled with stars,
Trees all around me,
What a beautiful night.
A water fountain,
With pure water rising,
The night is all mine.
How much better can it be,
But the moon shining
Down on me,
With the breeze of the air,
Rushing across my face,
No one around,
To talk,
To shout,
My world is as silent,
As can be,
This is my fantasy world.

Cemil Alkis (12)
Eastbury Comprehensive School

ISLAND POEM

I saw some baby tortoises
Making their way to the lovely sea.
I saw the crustaceans
On the bottom of the transparent sea.
I saw the sperm whales
Spraying the sea into the galaxy
I saw the sun lighting up the Earth.

Billy Parish (11)
Eastbury Comprehensive School

THE GREENEST PALM TREE

As I looked down on
the sparkling green palm tree
The sparkling deep blue sea
shone beside the greenest palm tree.
The brown coconuts softened
then became ripe.

As I slurped down the milk
out of the fresh coconut
in the golden sunshine,
the softest, creamiest clouds
passed by.

The little plane swooped into them
and blotches of cream were left in the sky.

Leigh-Anne Hayes (11)
Eastbury Comprehensive School

THE DREAM ISLAND

Soaked on a cloud flying over deep blue seas,
Over ridged mountains and valleys surrounded by trees.
On a pure white stallion galloping over hills,
The pounding hooves are noisy but the earth is deadly still.
On the back of a golden eagle soaring high above the world,
Discovering wondrous treasures - rubies, diamonds, pearls.
But then I am awoken by a bright moonbeam,
Shining through my window,
It was all just a dream.

Alex Ketley (12)
Eastbury Comprehensive School

ISLAND POEM

It was a sunny and beautiful day,
People were happy and gay.
People singing, people laughing,
It must be a summer's day.
Seagulls flying everywhere,
Making noises loud and clear.
What an island this could be,
If we had a VCR with a TV.

Neil Matthews (12)
Eastbury Comprehensive School

KALEIDOSCOPE

Colour so bright and dazzling
Shape so strong and clear
Magic of mixing colours

Amazing pictures in your mind
So near and yet so far
So clear and yet so hazy
Changing all the time

Never still
Seconds seem like hours
Minutes seem like days
A forever changing landscape
For a world that never ends.

Sarah Jones (12)
Gable Hall School

THE SCHOOL

The school is big
Big as can be.
Smart uniform so the teachers can see
Getting lost in the big wide school
Other pupils telling us how to find
English, science and the assembly hall.

It's so different from our junior school
You feel nervous, frightened and excited.
Lunchtime is great, you can eat in or out
So overall you can't compare your
Junior school to Gable Hall.

Laura Wiseman (11)
Gable Hall School

SCHOOL

G is for glad when I get home
A is for after school when I do my homework
B is for Bunsen burner that we use in science
L is for lunch the best part of the day
E is for English the best subject

H is for homework
A is for all of the lessons at school
L is for learning like we do
L is for Mr Longley because he is my form tutor.

Danny Stearn (11)
Gable Hall School

THE GHOST HOUSE!

You open the door,
You slowly walk in,
The door slams behind you,
As you fall like a pin.

You get ever so worried,
Your heart starts to pound,
You hear the werewolf,
The frightening hound.

He tries to get in,
You put a plank against the door,
He breaks the wood,
He claws him down, forever more.

The boy is dead,
He eats him up,
He leaves his bones,
Like a broken cup.

Adam Collins (11)
Gable Hall School

MY FIRST DAY AT GABLE HALL

The morning came
and I started to walk
I took a deep breath
and started to talk.
The bell rang twice
and I went inside,
Then all the teachers
said 'Hi.'

Then it came to break time,
and I took a deep breath,
Then I stepped outside
and I was shaking to death,
So am I big or am I small?
I'd better go and ask someone tall.
What I mean is when I see someone tall
I seem so little after all.

Charlene Ison (11)
Gable Hall School

FIRST DAY AT GABLE HALL

I walk through the gates with my friend,
Wondering if school will ever end.
I see my friends sitting in a group,
Then I realised they're not my friends,
The bell rang, it gave me a fright,
I walked into the school thinking
I must get everything right.
I was shown to my form room,
Hoping the day wouldn't go boom.
My new form tutor called out the register,
We all had to answer 'Yes Sir.'
I had music and English today,
There were eleven of us walking,
We were all talking,
After such a day
We really had to run away.
When I got home I put my feet up,
In the evening I put my alarm on early,
Do I have to get up?

Henna Gadhvi (11)
Gable Hall School

BEFORE AND AFTER!

Crack goes the trolley,
Scream goes the bell,
Out come the children,
Yell, yell, yell!

Chatting about everything,
About boys and all sorts of things,
Screaming, yelling, eating too!
So much food to choose from
What shall we choose
The noise is so loud
What can the teachers do?

Soon it's all peaceful
With plenty to do
The children are all quiet
The playground is too!

Kimberley Portas (14)
Gable Hall School

MY SCHOOL

G is for Gable Hall, our number one school,
A is for achievements gained in class,
B is for bully a menace of the past,
L is for learning the lessons we're taught,
E is for equality for both girls and boys,

H is for homework the key to success,
A is for ability, be it VIBS or YOGAR,
L is for listening, so as to learn,
L is for leisure at the end of term, *yippee!*

Steven Low (11)
Gable Hall School

THE TREASURE

In the park he goes
He sees a gang
Playing with yo-yos
He takes out a shiny toy
From his satchel
He sits down on the grass
He twists the end
Getting enjoyment out of it
The falling colours, creating shapes
The shapes change every time.

Now the other children stop playing
They come over to him
They want to know what's so much fun
He shows them his kaleidoscope
Now they put their yo-yos away
And take out the treasure.

Pamela Cox (15)
Gable Hall School

MY POEM ABOUT SCHOOL

I go to school at half past eight,
I ride my bike; I'm never late,
I park my bike in the shed,
Oh I wish I were still in bed,
At break time I go and get some tuck,
There's nothing there I'm out of luck,
It's dinnertime I'm in the mood,
All I want is some hot food,
It's twenty past three, the end of the day,
When I get home I will go out and play.

Adam Stevens (12)
Gable Hall School

THE PLAYGROUND

Before . . .
Burning tarmac
where seagulls land.
No one's there but
soon they'll stand.

The creak of a door,
the scrape of some wheels.
Out come the dinner ladies
with snacks and hot meals.

During . . .
The doors bang open
as people rush out.
Racing to the tuck queue
while they scream and shout.

Boys round the back
all playing football.
Everyone gathers as
they watch someone fall.

After . . .
Everyone's gone
you notice litter's been dropped.
The ground's been marked
where pigeons have plopped.

Biscuit wrappers
sandwich crusts.
Broken zips
beginning to rust.

All these things lay on the
playground floor.
As they sit and wait
for the kids once more.

Naomi Wilson (13)
Gable Hall School

THE PLAYGROUND

Quiet, peaceful, calm, undisturbed,
Footsteps of pupils can't be heard.
The seagulls speak in their own little voice
Only the slightest bit of noise,
By the fluttering and flying of the litter on the floor
Only the tiniest sound from the creaking door.

Then the bell rings and there's a great uproar,
Hundreds of feet treading the floor.
The noise and the scream of the 'ard' and 'sad' gangs.
The yelling, the shouting, the whistling and the bangs.
The short and long stories they have to share,
Some taking pride and a lot of care.
Taking the mickey out of the teachers they've had,
Telling who has been good and who has been bad.

Then, the bell rings and it's time to go in,
The children wishing the bell didn't ring.
But, now it's time, for them to get down to business,
Names of all kinds - Dan, Lee, Sue, Liz.
It may be boring but at the end of the day
You would prefer to work than to play!

Kirsty Osborne (13)
Gable Hall School

THE PLAYGROUND

Completely calm, no noise,
just silence, then suddenly
a sound of chatter, as the
dinner ladies wheel in the tuck food,
a ring of a bell, complete chaos.

Terribly noisy, loads of shouting
running towards the tuck queue,
discussions, groups standing around,
another ring of the bell.

The bell rang high pitched, it was
completely calm,
the silky white seagulls
swoop for the litter,
still no noise till lunchtime.

Christopher Flindall (13)
Gable Hall School

SPECTRUM OF COLOURS

If you look in the hole
deep down the long, long pole.
You will see an unusual pattern
red, blue, green, yellow,
colours shimmering brightly down the pole.

The multicoloured paper bits,
reflecting off the mirror.
Seems real, glamorous too.
You will only see it,
if you look down the Kaleidoscope.

Jackie Hon (12)
Gable Hall School

MAKING FRIENDS

On the first day of school
I met a boy called Paul.
We both made the trials
and now we play football.

On the second day of school
I met Paul in the corridor.
The first lesson was French
we found it quite a bore.

On the third day of school
Paul and I met at break.
We joined the tuck shop queue
the bell rang - we could not buy a cake.

On the fourth day of school
I met Paul in the hall.
We both had some grub
and then played handball.

On the final day of school
the bell rang at twenty past three.
Our first week of school was finished.
So bye bye from me . . .

Paul Lawford & Joel Ryder (11)
Gable Hall School

THAT MOUSE

The children look in the garden,
The children look in the house,
The children look all day long,
But where is that mouse?

He sees a lion prowling, searching for his food,
He sees a seagull flying swiftly through the air,
He sees a mother with her children coming home from school
He sees Humpty upon a wall,
Oh mousy tell him not to fall!

The children come in from the garden,
The children stay in the house,
For there on the table sat *that mouse*

Oh there you are mousy,
Where have you been?
Into a story book!
What have you seen?

Jennifer Starling (13)
Gable Hall School

THE PLAYGROUND

The line of people waiting
starving for their food.
As the door swung open
as people stuff their faces.
Food dropping
Litter floating
Boys running for their lives,
screaming, shouting even yelling.
Girls laughing in a group
boys' crowd playing football.

Bell rings
pushing, shoving, screaming, shouting
as people go to class.
As the line is empty
doors closed and the playground's full of seagulls.
Silent, quiet except for the rustle of leaves.
The empty playground . . .
screaming, shouting even yelling.

Kerri Donaldson (13)
Gable Hall School

PLAYGROUND

Pushing, shoving, screaming, shouting.
There goes the bell for lunch
eating, drinking, having fun
it's normal to everyone.

By 1.30pm the food has gone.
So now the games begin
pushing, shoving, screaming, shouting
it starts all over again.

The bell rings - everyone runs
back to where they came from.
The playground's dead and bare
with no one there except seagulls
so beware . . .

The only sound that can be heard
is the rustling of the leaves
and the sound of the birds.

Chris Hyde (13)
Gable Hall School

SLEEPING

Dreaming in my bed
thoughts in my head.
Thinking about the impossible
like being a lion (lethal).
I take a breath and sigh
in my warm bed I lie.
I keep saying to myself again and again
keep in bed for 3 months or if lucky
stay in for 10.
I hear some footsteps in the corridor.
Do they belong to my dad?
Only my brother sleep-walking.
Boy! Am I glad . . .
I hear my door creak
that shudders my thoughts.
Dreaming so many stories
I have never been taught.
My dad wakes me up
'Come on Will you fool!'
I wake up . . . see my clock
I'm late for school!

William Sparling (11)
Gable Hall School

TERRIBLE TUNNEL

Pushing, crashing
Such a fight
Pulling, crushing
Ever so tight
Battling, struggling
Got to get through
Crowding, swelling
Get through the crew
Cramming, bustling
Get to your class
Squashing, bashing
Ooh, watch the glass
Rushing, thumping
Finally there
Calming, slowing
Try again, if you dare.

David Bernie (11)
Gable Hall School

I'LL ALWAYS LOVE YOU . . .

I wake up in the morning and find
you there no more empty, a bedside is
left and I give a sigh and a moan.
I remember your gold and black fur
so shiny and fine, the way you let me
down with such ease but now you're a
memory locked behind a door in the
corner of my mind . . .

Stephen Pluck (13)
Gable Hall School

KALEIDOSCOPE

The ever changing patterns and pictures,
Never the same, never simple,
Like our complicated lives.
Moving around, forever shifting.
The smallest turn causes changes,
Sometimes colourful, vivid, bright.
Other times there is no light
Everything is dark and nothing
Can be seen clearly.
It is hard to predict what comes next,
Or remember everything that has been.
The future may be bright and colourful
Full of hope and dreams
Life is an ever changing kaleidoscope
Of fears, hopes and dreams.

Claire Bronze (14)
Gable Hall School

THE PLAYGROUND

Empty, peaceful, nobody around.
Until the noise of wheels is bound.
With dinner ladies out to come and see
the hungry faces waiting patiently.

As the bell goes, a rush for the queue,
the scrunch of the packets,
and smell of the food.
The children in groups, standing around
as the Year 11 prepare to stand their ground.

A huge sigh as the bell roars,
pick up the bags, and rush for the doors.
The playground is silent, also clear,
until school is out with a big cheer.

Louise Graves (13)
Gable Hall School

A POEM ABOUT HOMEWORK

Homework is . . .

As stinky as a skunk's tail
As vile as a rotten fish
As puzzling as Frankenstein's monster
As boring as your grandad's stories
As mad as a man in a straight jacket
As scary as your mum's underpants
As obvious as an unsolved question
As clear as fog
As stupid as a school child with a dunce's hat
As sweet as flour
As much fun as watching grass grow
As fascinating as Sir Elton John singing nursery rhymes
As enjoyable as shopping in a shoe store
As revolting as my grandma's black head
As tiring as running up and down one million steps
As nasty as playing rugby on concrete with no players.

Homework stinks . . . !

Oliver Jarvis (12)
Gable Hall School

TITANIC

The iceberg awaits,
The huge boat desperately turns,
A fatal large scrape.
Screams from lower decks,
Water pours through the huge scrape,
Deadly silence falls.
It started to sink,
To the vast ocean seabed,
Downwards to its grave.
Lifeboats were lowered,
Into the dark gloomy sea,
The ice-cold ocean.
Everyone rushes,
Scrambling to get the boats,
People die, souls lost.
The bubbles rose up,
As the Titanic went down,
Until seen no more.
Destiny awaits,
On the dark and misty seabed.
The legend lives on.

Chris Leverett & Chris Solari (13)
Gable Hall School

POEM

Shiny pieces of paper
they dance all day.
The light is like a rhythm
as they swing and sway . . .

K Nevard (11)
Gable Hall School

BULLYING

I was being bullied
I was all alone.
I had no one to turn to
I was on my own.
My friends were against me
I had nowhere to go.
I needed someone to talk to
to tell of my woe.
I phoned Childline on 0800 1111
they told me what I should've done.
They've left me alone
Now I can play
Thank you Childline, you saved my day . . .

Nicola Bessell & Jemma Clarke (13)
Gable Hall School

SCHOOL

When I went to school
I thought I looked like a fool.
In uniform shining black.
I got split up from the pack.

Into a class of many new faces.
All from so many different places.
For every corridor that I turn
there's a different subject for me to learn.

Teachers, pupils, everywhere
I have no time to stop and stare.
My pupil Fax is by my side
the opportunities to learn are wide.

Graeme Silcock (11)
Gable Hall School

THE CLOUD

Far away in the distance
I see a cloud go by.
It's just like life I think
floats about and passes by.

I sometimes think that I'm a cloud
covering the brightness of the sun.
Then pour down rain of sadness
I'm sorry for the wrong.

Maybe I'm no truth of life
maybe I'm the lie.
Maybe I belong in hell
where I can cry and cry.

Then as a cloud I disappear
the light shines down on you.
Happiness is now very near.
Now the cloud has gone.

Sorry is not enough
I thank you for not giving up.
Hopefully the cloud will cease
the sun can shine again . . .

Danielle Stobbs (13)
Gable Hall School

THE PLAYGROUND

The playground is silent,
trees blow as the silent wind passes.
Seagulls fly in the empty space.

The bell rings, the playground is crowded
people stand laughing and crying.
Crowds form shouting and pushing.
Playtime has finished.

The playground is empty,
litter covers the floor.
Seagulls swarm searching for food,
crunching, flapping.
The food is eaten -
The playground is silent . . .

Lee Wightwick (13)
Gable Hall School

THE DARKNESS FROM WITHIN

What humanity is there left
In our hearts, our minds, our souls?
A darkness prevents our salvation
And is escaping through our minds.
Now the beast has confronted me
I know not what to do.
His putrid darkness, sinister but yet enticing
Is growing through our minds and thoughts
And unless we stand up to his power
We all shall soon be caught.

Alex Blewer (15)
Gaynes School

CATS

Cats, cats
they are everywhere
in every corner
of every street
there will be a cat
giving you its frightening glare
be careful and try not to
return its stare.

With its big green round eyes
and long black fury tail.
Claws cleverly hidden
as it creeps along its hidden trail.

Cats, cats
they are everywhere.
Prowling the streets with
their ears propped up high.
The wind blowing the trees
from side to side.
Leaves rustling a ghostly sigh
and the dustbin lids rattling
enticing, teasing, saying
'Come look inside me for those
fishy bones and tasty treats.'

As they prowl the streets at night
and slowly creep along
the high fences and walls
staring down at the hollow ground.

Spying for any lost food which can
be found.
Silently they wait watching for
their prey.
Suddenly without warning they
pounce without delay.

Michelle Groom (14)
Gaynes School

I'M ONLY A DOG . . .

I'm only a dog
I have no one to care for me.
My family kick me . . . push me.
They don't care for me.
They don't walk me.
They don't even talk to me.
They shout at me like I'm deaf.
The other day I cut my foot on some glass.
Crunch! It went, I yelped in pain.
They wouldn't even take me to the vet!
They said I was just a dumb old pet.
There is a nine year old boy
Who uses me as his toy.
In summertime
They run off and leave me.
They lock me up and they don't even leave a key.
Nobody can save me.
So all I can do is curl up and die.
So I'll go away and leave you now . . . goodbye.

Linzee McCutcheon (13)
Gaynes School

THE GIANT SPIDER

Being a spider isn't easy.
So small, so defenceless, so vulnerable.
Not like the giants, no one picks on them.
Crawling on endless stretches of slippery
clumps of soft matted wool.
Not like the giants, no one picks on them.

I like sitting in the bath tub
but even then I get washed away into darkness.
Not like the giants, no one picks on them.
I sometimes feel safer, high up on the ceiling.
But even then they reach me,
wherever I am, whatever I do . . .
Not like the giants, no one picks on them.

Samantha Butler (13)
Gaynes School

THE GOLDFISH

How I'd hate to be a goldfish
stuck inside the old murky dish.
Although to be quite dim
there's no room for a fish to swim.

How he'd like to live in the sea
where all the humans can leave him be.
But all he wants is a mate
to give a little love and hate.

But that goldfish is still
stuck inside that old murky dish . . .

John Bradley (13)
Gaynes School

DOLPHIN FROM THE DEEP

The deep azure blue ocean, shining like a jewel.
The sun sparkling down on the speckled white foam.
The song of a dolphin rings out loud and clear.
In the water he dances, dances, alone.

The waves become rocky
as a fishing ship rears straight ahead.
The dolphin underneath the ocean
hears the noise and leaves his water bed.

The dolphin dances, daintily diving
as the ship ploughs its way through
the foam flecked furrows.
Bang! A net crashes down into the spiky waves,
just as the dolphin dives into its watery burrow.

The dolphin, its curiosity taking over,
gracefully swims up to the net.
Inside it can see a tuna fish meal
hunger overcomes fear, needing to be met.

Then suddenly the nets are clasped around him
and the dolphin is vulnerable to the enclosing twine.
He wriggles and jumps and tries to squirm his way free,
but he is frightened, fearful and flounders as he
thrashes in the brine.

Up on the boat, nowhere to float.
Nowhere to swim or see.
So the dolphin can call all he likes
but no one will come to set him free.

Fiona Clare (13)
Gaynes School

WAITING FOR DINNER

She stretches her small padded paws after
that lovely long sleep.
In the distance she sees a mouse crawl
quickly along the carpet.
Her claws spring out.
Her small pink mouth yawns showing those
sharp dagger teeth ready for the attack.
She walks slowly and quietly to the mouse's
hiding place.
Meow, meow . . .
Her glossy coat shining in the light.
Her shoulder blades moving.
Her sleek fur stretching.
A secret detective was what she was like.
She makes it to the hiding place without the
mouse noticing her.
Into the dark corner she lays and waits and waits.
Her green eyes with deep black pupils stare into the dark hole.
No one knows when the mouse will come out
but you can be certain that when it does decide to,
she will be there . . . ready for the attack.

Laura Marshall (13)
Gaynes School

TORTOISE

Tortoise, tortoise, in your shell
why can't you tell
what it's like in your shell.
Is it heaven or is it hell?
Oh, why can't you tell.
Tortoise, tortoise in your shell

Michael Fenn (13)
Gaynes School

WHALES

Whales should be free to swim and play
not kept in a small old tank all day.
When you see whales playing in the sea.
You think 'Wouldn't it be lovely
to be happy and free?'
The whales I know are black
and white.
And when you see them
you want to squeeze them tight.
So don't capture whales and
make them suffer.
They want to dive and hunt for
their supper . . .

Laura Howes (14)
Gaynes School

CHAMELEON

As I watch my prey
with my big bubbling and bulging eyes.
Still as a statue - the prey is my lunch.
I have two more catches.
It means I am a shark hunting my food
with green leaves behind me in the way of camouflage.
I am the gleaming green grass of spring.
As I am ready to pounce out my tongue.
It goes silent as a mouse.
Slurp goes my tongue, as it pulls my food back in.
Just before I go, I spot my next piece of food
'*Yum! Yum!*

Paul Coombe (13)
Gaynes School

SLITHERY SNAKES

Those slithery snakes make my skin crawl.
Some people say they're more scared of you
but I personally think that's not true.
You see them in zoos
behind the glass
but you're still fearful even though
they're hiding in the grass.

I sometimes have dreams of thousands
of them in my bed.
It's terrible, but I can't get this thought
out of my head.

Why on earth has God given us
these long, slimy, ugly, slithery creatures?
I hate their eyes, the way they stare
back at you!
My brother says he wants to get a few.
I don't detest other animals . . .
It's just those slithery, slimy, snakes.

Alex Tucker (13)
Gaynes School

WHALING

The whales that swim so peacefully in the deep blue sea.
They hunt and trap these poor creatures.
Just so they can receive a hefty fee.
Their eyes are so shiny along with all their features.

The whales are killed and cruelly slaughtered
The hurt and dismay in this creature's eyes.
Don't you think it's about time things were altered?
They look for their blubber as the poor whale dies.
The beautiful big blubber beasts are pound signs.

They tie the whale tightly with a rope.
The relatives of the whale surely have no hope.
How can whales trust us at all?
And if they do . . . they're heading for a fall.

Nicola Kelly (13)
Gaynes School

A CAT HAS FEELINGS

I was left in a box with two other cats.
Yes I thought I've been found a good home
someone will want me and love me.
The other cats are gone I'm alone . . . no-one wants me.

Then I heard some news, someone wants me.
I see the people who want me, I cannot wait to go home.
I'm home, everyone is there, they love me.
I think I'm going to love it here, a very good home.

I love it when they cuddle me
I can feel love in the house.
It's so nice here, everyone cares for me
wherever I am people are caring for me.

The dogs they seem to really love me too
the big one lets me play on him.
We have fun all day playing, then sleeping.
I don't want to leave here, I just want to stay.

I'm as happy as a dog with a new bone.
I'm just happy to have a second chance to live.

Charlotte Till (13)
Gaynes School

CATS AND TEARS

Meow-Meow was a precious cat.
He lived with us for years.
He chose us by walking in one day.
In the middle of my sister's tears.

She'd been crying you see
because we'd lost our dog.
He died the previous week
the tears had been raining down since then.
Till Meow-Meow brushed past her cheek.

We didn't know from whence he came
and we tried to locate his home.
But we never found out - so Meow-Meow stayed
but he always seemed alone.

My sister was his closest friend
till one day we realised our fears.
For Meow-Meow - had gone
the same way that he came . . .
In the middle of my sister's tears.

Katie Drakard (13)
Gaynes School

HUNTED

Swarming with flies and coated in red
hunted and killed for the things on its head.

Do you honestly think that they're rightfully yours
to prance and show off then hang on the doors?
They're too big to handle, they're pointy and round
shooting till death then just leave on the ground.

Crying like a human in fear and in pain
falling tears from a soldier - a soldier in shame.
Sons and daughters - how will they cope?
Now that he's dead what is there but hope!

We were once a herd - wild and keen.
Now guns and humans are rotten and mean.

*So please you humans stop following us
we are only elephants and we need our tusks . . .*

Kerrie Game (13)
Gaynes School

A DOLPHIN'S DAY

D ucking diving in the brine a Dolphin's day is so divine
O ver and under the waves they go
L ike dancers in their show
P laying merrily with the rest
H owever can we doubt that dolphins are the best
I gnorant are they of their shrinking world
N ow their day is almost done
S plashing, singing, your soulful song is sung.

Antonia Cooper (13)
Gaynes School

THE ELEPHANT

Wrinkled grey with little hair,
Most of the time I stand and stare.
Long, straight legs,
a tail with a tuft reaching to the ground,
flapping ears,
to keep cool.
Bathing in mud,
playing the fool.
A trunk to use like a hand,
smelling, breathing,
picking up things from the land.

A mother feeding her calf,
giving him milk.
Watching him grow,
eating grass,
Chewing leaves,
playing.
Ever watchful of man,
The hunter.

Man's greed for ivory
Will destroy us . . .

Richard Keegan (13)
Gaynes School

WHO'S HUNTING WHO

He's hunted by day
he hunts at night.
Against the hounds and horsemen
he puts up a fight.

He hunts to survive
they hunt for fun.
He slows for a rest
then moves quickly
at the noise of a gun.

The hunt is to control them
so that's what they say.
A rich man's hobby
golf the next day.

They are chased from the wild
into the city.
Then reported as pests.
It seems such a pity.

The debates, the confusion
the fighting, the pain.
And still nothing sorted
it seems all in vain.

Still being hunted throughout the day
at night he will scavenge and hunt out his prey.
Smelling for rabbits, chickens and sheep
searching through bins, black bags an old box.

Just instinctively doing
The defenceless fox . . .

Danny Norton (13)
Gaynes School

PIGS

On the farm you can smell the smell
from which you can really tell
the only animals that they keep
are large and pink and roll around in mud.

The home they have is called a sty.
The aroma they have will make your eyes cry.
They eat all they can of any old food
it is mixed up until it goes soft.
The farmer then puts it in their trough.

They're big, long and round
and you should hear their sound.
They snort and grunt
the smallest is called a *runt*.
Pigs don't move very fast, they plod and shuffle.
Unless food is involved then they run and scuffle.

They spend their days eating and sleeping,
exercise is not in their keeping.
The most they do is get up and eat
then it's time for another treat.
That's to sleep in mud . . . oh, glorious mud!

Danielle Rawlinson (13)
Gaynes School

Sweet Sheep . . .

Well everyone knows that sheep go *baa*
and the little sheep go *baa* too.
But when sheep sleep
you won't hear them peep
because they sound like a little parked car.
I always say that sheep are sweet
and the little sheep are sweet too.
You'll always here a sheep go *baa*
but never hear a sheep go *moo*!

Nicola Watson (13)
Gaynes School

The Shipwreck

The ship, the ship,
turned over in the night,
the roaring sound,
as the ship went down.

Floating down beneath the ground,
the sharks were circling,
round and round.

I was crying,
as the ship went down,
my heart was beating round and around,
it was then I thought, I was going to drown.

Lauren Saunders (12)
Harold Hill Community School

THE KING OF THE JUNGLE

There they are,
There they are,
They sparkle in the moonlight,
When it is so bright,
The king of the jungle and the night.
I can't believe what I once saw,
The most wonderful thing,
Goldish brown but very dangerous,
They prowl and hunt for the best
Meal of the night.
They will come and catch us
But not if we catch them first
The lion, the best and no-one
But me has seen this wonderful
Animal and his very goldish hair.
Be fair to this animal or,
He won't be fair to you.

Michelle Perfect (13)
Harold Hill Community School

TIGERS

Tiger in the grass
eyes staring at its prey.
Jumps and kills it fast
watches it bleed while it lays.

Tiger on the tree trunk
claws dug in tight.
Watching its prey
shivering with fright.

The sun slowly disappears
as he settles off to sleep.
He lies down and his eyelids drop
then the cubs pile on top.

To end my poem
I'd like to say.
Look after these beautiful creatures
care for them day by day.

Terri Johnson (12)
Harold Hill Community School

THE STORM

Standing on the shore
alone by the sea.
The wind is picking up
it's cold as cold can be.

The trees are bending over
the sea is getting rough.
I'm starting to weaken
now I'm not so tough.

Now I'm getting scared
I want to run and hide.
I want to escape the terror
the trees, the waves, the tides.

Finally, I've found some shelter
underneath the ground.
Covered myself in leaves and stuff,
I could hide there all year round.

Carla Wheeler (12)
Harold Hill Community School

THE ISLAND

The island is swaying,
side to side,
While the water is pushing
and pulling either side.
The shore is as calm as the sea.

While it is at its calmest time,
As I sit on the golden sand,
I see the sunlight sparkling
on the sea.

The time is half past four,
The birds start to sing
more and more,
As I start to see that the
island is as beautiful as me.

Martin Hartshorn (12)
Harold Hill Community School

DOLPHIN

The dolphin swims with grace and ease,
he flips and jumps the crowd to please.
They clap and cheer with great delight,
the trainer assures he will not bite.
His playful nature, will win your heart
and remember him as you depart.
The day may come when he is no more.
This gentle giant of the deep
will close his eye in an endless sleep.

Chantelle Smith (11)
Harold Hill Community School

ENDLESS WAR

The marching soldiers weary of the endless fighting.
Walk across the vast battlefield toward the muddy trenches
which they have spent too long in, always praying
for an end to the slaughter.

The bombs drop, the guns fire
never stopping for a moment of silence or calm.
Whilst enemy swords clash and cannons fire.
Whilst soldiers die for their country
the Generals sit and decide who is to die next.

Gas bombs and mines kill those
who do not deserve to die such a terrible death.
The huge tanks towering against the sky
crushing any unlucky enough to be in their way.

The carnage and horror of war
where Death stalks at leisure.
His bony fingers holding the sharp glinting scythe.
Taking the souls of whom he pleases
and leaving the rest to suffer.

The screams of the dying soldiers
left to die, alone and afraid.
The guns which have spilled enough blood
to turn the oceans red.
When will they finally fire their last?

Clare Eddington (15)
Harold Hill Community School

MY WAR POEM

Jet planes flew
cluster bombs dropped.
Terrible carnage
heavy tanks crushed mud underneath its tracks.

Nervous Privates ordered out,
continuous enemy fire.
They run
slow ones get caught
bloody death.

Big Navy ships move in.
They stop
fire their missiles,
frightening explosions.

Nuclear submarines ready to fire
locked on target.
Fire!
Direct hit!
Enemy ship blown up.

Scared commander
radios for help.
Relieved allies as reinforcements come
strong soldiers throw grenades.
Over enemy lines,
screams of dying enemy soldiers
echoes for miles.

Charge! The Army moves over the line
into no-mans land.
With guns blazing.

Will the fighting ever stop?

Warren Pearce (16)
Harold Hill Community School

HURRICANE

Winds start blowing
sea gets rough.
Sky gets black
clouds come over
winds blow harder.
Trees sway from side to side.
They are like rubber that's really easy to bend.
The wind roars like lions hungry and angry.
People run under the shelters they have made
barely staying on the ground.
It's all over . . .
Shelters wrecked and trees all bent.
Messy floors and sky clears up
It's all over . . .

Hayley Fitzpatrick (13)
Harold Hill Community School

HURRICANE

The light blue sky
was calm and peaceful.
But then the clouds started
to swirl and light up the grey sky.
The winds were swirling high
like a big bird in the sky.
The trees began to blow from side to side.
The trees began to whistle
and take from the ground.
The terror of terror was here again.

Billy Fisher
Harold Hill Community School

THE CROSS COUNTRY

It's nearly time to start my run
but people think it's only fun.
I've now warmed up, and focused hard
I'm ready, set to play my card.

Bang . . . !

The gun goes off, I'm pushing past
I know I mustn't go too fast.
It's a long old haul up the hill
but sprinting off is against my will.

I edge my way towards the front
I know I mustn't take the brunt.
The cold wet mud around my feet
a long hot shower would be a treat.

It's through those woods and around the bend
will this race ever end?
My heart is beating fit to burst
my legs are feeling even worse.

The cheering crowds edge me on
all at once my legs feel strong.
It's time for me to take the lead
I'm now determined to succeed.

I see the finish now in sight
I now excel with all my might.
I'm now in first about to win
It's *gold* for me . . . I sure do grin.

Selena Humphryes (15)
Harold Hill Community School

HOUSE OF PARENTS

In my house of parents we
have lots to do,
Get rid of pets and get more too,
Sing my poem through and through,
We have lots to do,
Paint the rooms up and down,
Paint them round and listen
to the sound,
Time to go to bed,
Get rid of my sleepy head,
Get up in the morning,
By 8 o'clock I'm still yawning,
We still have lots to do,
Phew!

Cheryl Fuller (11)
Harold Hill Community School

CROCODILES

C laws like daggers
R eady to grab
O n the bank he creeps along
C rouching down green and strong
O nly he knows who he'll eat
D on't go near him you may lose your feet
I n the grass he does hide
L urking around at high tide
E veryone is scared of him
S o don't even think about going for a swim.

Nicky Gildersleve (11)
Harold Hill Community School

MARY JONES

There once was a lady called Mary Jones
who at the age of 79.
Lived on the streets of Hammersmith
and didn't look too fine.

She's what you call a *bag-lady*
That means she has no home.
She carried her things with her
everywhere she roamed.

Her only friend was a dog called Charles
Like Mary - really old.

One night at Aldgate Station
with her dearest friend.
Looking through rubbish bins
the dog's hair stood on end.

He'd heard a rustling, scraping noise
which Mary then heard too.
The noise was getting closer
stopped and then resumed.

More strange noises
a beeping sound.
Hypnotised Mary
and was never found.

All that was found of Mary
were her clothes (not brand new).
But the only strange thing was
they were all covered in *goo*!

Stewart Piercy (12)
Harold Hill Community School

TUBE DISASTER

Mary Jones is homeless
she finds coins and mobile phones.
She has a dog called Charles
if he's lucky, he might get a bone.
They live in Hammersmith, London,
she goes every night to Aldgate Tube Station.

One night they did as normal.
Hunting for money and other valuables.
She got coins, lighters and mobile phones
luckily for her she didn't find any marbles.
She heard a rustling and a bustling down the tunnel
like a bat, Mary and Charles ran flat.

The next night they were down at Aldgate
they were nowhere near the gate.
Charles ears propped
Mary's legs flopped
They went down the tunnel that night
and had a big fright . . .

John Rowland (12)
Harold Hill Community School

SPURS

S ol Campbell goes on his run down the wing and
P uts a cross in and an
U nexpected goal.
R oars of cheering as
S uper scoring Armstrong has done it again.

Darren Gooding (11)
Harold Hill Community School

THE POEM ABOUT MY ISLAND

The island is so small
But the waves are so big
We see the dolphins diving down
Like they have to dig.

The sand sparkles in the sun
Like a polished crystal
But when the tide goes out
All is silent and calm.

When the sun goes down
And wildlife goes to sleep
Everything remains still
But that is for the better.

Craig Ling (13)
Harold Hill Community School

FEELINGS

The sun rose
through the dirty air
with traces of light
almost everywhere
the rain was drowsy
and the wind was strong
but the sprinkles of love
were all among.

David Dean (12)
Harold Hill Community School

THE SEA

The sea is like a mirror
it glistens in the sun.
People like to swim in it
and have a lot of fun.

The fish are red
The fish are blue
The fish are yellow
and I am too!

There are a lot of sea animals
that snap at your feet.
Some you want to see
Some you don't want to meet.

I could see the seagulls
flying over me.
Then they dived down and down
right into the sea.

I dived right into the sea
and the fish were around me.

Tracey Lamb (13)
Harold Hill Community School

MY NAME

R oss plays basketball all day long.
O atmeal makes me fit and strong.
S ome people think I'm thick and wrong.
S o tell them to move *along.*

Ross Loan (11)
Harold Hill Community School

THE THING

There was Mary Jones
she was seventy nine.
She had no house
nothing on which to dine.

She had only a dog for company
Charles was his name.
He enjoyed picking up junk with Mary
he liked the game.

Once at the train station
Mary had just picked up a cup.
Charles began growling
then his fur suddenly pricked up.

They heard a sound from the tunnel
they shivered as they stood there listening.
An eerie sound they heard
it was the sound of paper rustling.

The next night it happened again
they heard again the noise.
She grabbed her bag and searched
searched through coins and toys.

'Aha!' she screamed.
As she pulled out a cigarette lighter.
Down the tunnel she saw some objects
which now appeared brighter.

She saw two segmented ovals
floating in the air.
They seemed to be hypnotising
so they walked over there.

Mary walked up the tunnel
Charles went up too.
Their only remains were
blobs of goo . . . !

Adam Carman (13)
Harold Hill Community School

LIFE ON THE ISLAND

Shimmer, shine the waters
sparkling like the sun and stars,
like the raindrops coming down
from the sky.

The sand is imitating the dust
and dirt of an old western movie,
blowing away to a part we have
never seen.

The growth of plant life is incredible
the jungle of the wild, who dares to go in?
Not me . . .

But now is night and time to rest my eyes.
Now the sea is black, black as ebony.
The sand is white from the reflection
of moonlight.

And the jungle is quiet but still dark
and even more interesting to explore
but for now I'll put it on hold.
Goodnight! Goodnight!
Goodnight . . . !

Laura Everingham (12)
Harold Hill Community School

TROPICAL POEM

The sun, the sun, the sun
was shining down on me.
The great red crabs glistening
running by my feet.

The palm trees overlapped
slapping each other
clap, clap, clap!
With the bugs, the birds and the bees
buzzing above the shore.
The waves were roaring, shouting,
swish, swish, swee!

Dolphins diving over waves by wave.
Screaming and screeching
at the deep blue sea.
With tropical fish
glick, glick, gliding!

There were rocks here and there
brown and black with waves crashing
upon them with a *splash, splash, splat.*

I'm here on my own
Silent maybe
Sitting under a palm tree
beside the sea.
Nothing to fear
I shed another
tear, tear, tear!

Kirsty May (12)
Harold Hill Community School

THE ISLAND POEM

There is not a lot to eat
the fruit's so sweet.
I don't like much else
definitely not the animals.

Some parts are dangerous
so I told the rest don't go.
They kept asking me
but I just said no!

The water is near
it's also clean
I like it because it's clear
It has got to be the best place
I've been to . . .

Garry Richards (12)
Harold Hill Community School

HURRICANE

The sky was blue,
So was the sea,
Also quiet,
As quiet as can be.

A big strong wind,
Started to come,
The sea was lashing and lashing away.

We figured out what it was,
Because we heard the whistling wind,
And there it was, a twirling blast of wind.

Tony Marcham (12)
Harold Hill Community School

HURRICANE 1951

I saw it coming straight from the North Sea
It was very huge, as big as the sky,
especially when it moved.

The sky had turned completely black
and the waves were tall as could be,
but I had to keep myself cool and calm,
otherwise it would get me.

The trees were shaking as fast as ever
and it was very very scary,
but that very moment I saw a log
coming straight towards me.

The noise of the storm was all I could hear,
but I knew that they were very normal,
some of the sounds were loud and soft
but still didn't help me at all.

The shelter wasn't that great,
but at that very moment the sounds had stopped
and the storm was finally over,
and if you ask me it was for the better.

Scott Bines (12)
Harold Hill Community School

THE HURRICANE

I noticed the trees,
bend to the side,
I knew it was bad when,
I saw the tide.

The sky went black,
like a blot of ink,
The sea went deep blue,
what would happen, I could not bear to think.

The trees looked like,
broken umbrellas,
and I knew what
it was trying to tell us.

The wind was howling,
as the rain came down,
The thunder sounded,
like a pound, pound, pound.

We decided not to go in the shelter,
because of the storm's lighting,
We knew to go to a clearing,
but that was really frightening.

When I got up,
from the ground,
The place was a wreck,
and no shelter I found.

Stuart Craske (12)
Harold Hill Community School

THE ISLAND

The island is big
like the sun
The sea is like a never-ending story
The sea shines in the sun
And at the bottom of the sea
There's a deep blue secret
Waiting to be let out
The green grass is overgrown
like a forest, big, green and brown
The colours light up day by day
At night they go away
I see the birds flying
Swiftly in the blue sky
I see the monkeys climbing
I feel I'm not alone
But then I realise I'm on my own.

Daniel Connely (13)
Harold Hill Community School

DRACULA

The count
The tall count
The tall evil count
The tall evil pale count
The tall evil pale count flies
The tall evil pale count flies freely
The tall evil pale count flies freely through the sky
The tall evil pale count flies freely
through the midnight sky.
The tall evil pale count flies freely
through the dark midnight sky.

Vicky Lee (13)
Harold Hill Community School

COMMENDATION

'*C* an we have a commendation Miss?'
'*O* h no, you can't'
'*M* iss please'
M any people want them but they can't have them
E ven though they beg the teachers they
N ever give them out
D ay by day
A nd week by week
T he teachers do not let us have them
I n order to get them we have to work
O ur fingers are falling off at the end of the day
N ever mind, it's out to play.

Andrew Yeomans (12)
Harold Hill Community School

THE BUTTERFLIES

Can you see the butterflies
Eating all the apple pies?
'Leave them alone' I do say
'Eat something else - not that, I pray'
'Stop that or I'll eat you alive'
'That's not nice so do I get a surprise?'
'Eat something else' I say
'Be back until another day'
'Read a book you horrible child
Or you'll be dumb at school or blind'
We will go on forever more, but have to go
Not no more.

Celeste Brown (12)
Harold Hill Community School

THE SHIP

The bosun is the man that screams
the tiny boy who has those dreams

The captain is the big bad boss
the one with boots who is always cross

The cabin boy is a small little lad
sometimes one with but a dad

The look-out post is tall and thin
the huge flag mast is lined with tin

The hammock beds are very small
but are attached upon a wall.

Robert Harris (13)
Harold Hill Community School

I DIDN'T DO MY HOMEWORK BECAUSE . . . !

I didn't do my homework because I went out
I didn't do my homework because it was too hard
I didn't do my homework because my pen ran out
I didn't do my homework because my dog chewed it up
I didn't do my homework because I couldn't be bothered
I didn't do my homework because I forgot to write it down

I didn't do my homework because . . . um . . . well that's it.

Natalie Sanderson (15)
Harold Hill Community School

My Best Friend Is An Alien

My best friend is an alien,
She comes from outer space,
She came down from her spaceship
With a smile upon her face.

My best friend is an alien,
I know it's rather strange,
She's from another planet,
But I don't want her to change.

My best friend is an alien,
I know it must sound weird,
She wants to keep it secret,
Being found out is what she fears.

My best friend is an alien,
She helps me out a lot,
She gets me out of trouble,
When I'm put on the spot.

My best friend is an alien,
She's the greatest friend there is,
She can do lots of cool and funny tricks,
She really is a whiz.

My best friend is an alien,
She can be your friend too,
All you need's imagination,
For of course it isn't true.

Nichola Aldridge (11)
Hassenbrook School

CHRISTMAS

Christmas is the time of year,
when snow falls there and here,
the crisp white snow glistens in the sun,
there's fun and joy for everyone,
all day long I can see,
boys and girls playing gleefully.

Lots of presents for girls and boys,
things like sweets, chocolate and toys,
lie beneath the Christmas tree,
waiting to be opened by you or me,
so happy Christmas everyone,
I hope you enjoy it and have some fun.

Jennifer Taylor (11)
Hassenbrook School

MATES

Mates are what I call fun,
All my *mates* are number one.
We play together every day,
Except for one who lives far away.
I always phone and say hello,
Then I say I have to go.
My *mates* are knocking on the door,
We're going to have some fun and more.
Us *mates* we like to muck about,
We like to jump, talk, sing and shout.
We have our rows and our doubts,
But that's what friendship's all about!

Ashley King (11)
Hassenbrook School

SEVEN STARS

Silver moonlight
Sparkling stars
Forgetting the noises
Of buses and cars

Silence is golden
As the people say
Looking at the sky at night
Forgetting my busy day

Lying on the dewy grass
Is my idea of heaven
I always count the stars
Tonight there are seven.

Katie Jackson (11)
Hassenbrook School

DOLPHINS

You sometimes see them if you're lucky,
Swishing through the deep blue sea.
Up and down having fun,
But only happy if there's more than one.
They're meant to be friendly,
Kind and gentle.
They're meant to have silky skin,
So there are my reasons
For liking dolphins,
Swishing through the deep blue sea.

Hayleigh Kelway (11)
Hassenbrook School

THE WHITE HORSE

She gallops through the grass-filled fields,
She travels past the workers' mills.

She finds a spot to spend the night,
Her coat is shining not black but white.

Her eyes are soft and brown,
She lays there quietly not a sound.

Her spirit free, her sail is calm,
There is no need for a quick alarm.

She's getting old,
But she's not sold.

She still lives free,
For me to see.

The old white horse she still lives on,
Her soft quiet whinnies are like a song.

She now has a foal,
With the same kind of soul.

And she looks just like her mother,
With a white gleaming cover.

I watch her baby now run free,
She is still there for me to see.

Kelly Mackenzie (11)
Hassenbrook School

MY BEST HOLIDAY

I had a holiday in the sun
It was really, really fun,
I went with my sister, my mum and my dad,
We went to a restaurant and we had,
Burgers and chips and all things nice,
But my mum and my dad had curry and rice,
Me, my mum, my dad and my sis,
Went to a place called Alonissos,
We had fun and shopped all day,
Then we got lost and couldn't find our way,
We went swimming and had a little munch,
then we went out and had some lunch,
We go out at night for a drink,
and when I'm out that's when I think,
This is the best holiday *ever!*

Hannah Grover (11)
Hassenbrook School

MY DOG, MY FRIEND

Someone to welcome me
when I come home
A comforting paw
when I'm feeling alone
A faithful companion
loving and true
To comfort and welcome me
all the day through
All this I've found
in a friend as friendly as you.

Laura Kruppa (12)
Hassenbrook School

SUTTON HALL FARM TEAM

I live next to the stables
The girls they are quite odd
There's Joy, Nic, Kim, Lisa,
Barbara, Tracy, Nod.

Nod's old man is Richie
He's quite a funny guy
He often makes them laugh so much
That they begin to cry.

Now to mention Barbara
Barbara Tea should be her name
She's always making cups of tea
Again, again, *again!*

Kim, she has a little girl
(Laura is her name)
She rides a long-haired hippie horse
Oscar is his name.

Nic they call the Cat Lady
For her care of cats
The one good thing that they do best
Is catching all the rats.

Tracy is the owner
She's the one in charge
She keeps it nice and tidy
It's a lovely looking yard.

They really are a happy gang
The girls that are next door
I only wish that I could go
Over there much more.

Daniel Coote (11)
Hassenbrook School

MOVING AWAY

Empty room
and all too soon
this our home
is all alone

cupboards bare
an empty chair
curtains drawn
an unmown lawn

uncarpeted floor
a creaking door
sad today
we're moving away.

Loren Havey (11)
Hassenbrook School

IF I WON THE LOTTERY

If I won the lottery
I know what I would do
I'd spread it all around the world
From here to Timbuktu
It could feed all the children
And teach them how to read
And give them all the other things
That they really need
When the money has all gone
And the children have been fed
I know that we can all go home
To our comfy bed.

Sarah Woodward (12)
Hassenbrook School

ANONYMOUS

She has such blonde hair
And such big blue eyes
Her skin is so fair
So where does beauty lie?

The looks she gets
I see the desire in their eyes
What am I missing?
So where does beauty lie?

Should I change my style?
Perhaps look deep within
Or should I be myself?
So where does beauty lie?

Do I sound envious?
Should I feel jealous?
Am I not gorgeous?
Am I sad?
Oh where does beauty lie?

I know I'm not bad
And know I'm not sad
I know I have beauty within
I'm happy with my appearance

I want love, not lust

I know where beauty lies - *inside!*

Rebecca Singleton (15)
Hassenbrook School

THE START OF THE DAY

Still dark, Mum's call.
'Come on Sarah, time for school.
Laura, James, it's getting late
Shake a leg - it's nearly eight.'

Down we go, breakfast served
Mum's in a panic
Haven't you heard
'I've got to work to make ends meet
Get dad up, upon his feet.

Tell him to dress Laura Jade
Her clothes are ironed
Her lunch is made

I haven't time to wait around
Work awaits, so I pound
See ya kids after school
Here comes dad, and he will rule.'

Dad appears, face all glum
'Come on Sarah, come on son
Stop that Laura, sit on the mat
Take your fingers off the cat.'

I'll be glad when I'm in school
Teachers shouting, teachers call
I hope I will be on the ball
Learning lessons in my school.

The moral of this story I will relate
Get up early and you won't be late.

Sarah Stannard (12)
Hassenbrook School

FOOD

I'm sitting here
Deciding on verse
I'm getting hungry
So it might get worse.

I like pizza,
I like chips,
Especially with
Some salad and dips.

Tomatoes are scrummy,
Potatoes are nice,
Mix them together,
And add some rice.

I don't like liver,
Nor baked beans,
I think they're gross,
And so are sardines.

Pasta is slimy,
Chillies are hot,
You can have them,
But I'd rather not.

Cornflakes are OK,
So are the rest,
But a good English breakfast,
Is always the best.

I like ice-cream,
Yoghurts and cakes,
Especially the ones,
That my mum makes.

I'm sitting here,
With my mum making tea,
I've got to go now,
It's right in front of me.

Emma Holding (12)
Hassenbrook School

SCHOOL

It's half seven
And the school is alone
It's standing in the dawn
Waiting for the sun to be born
It suddenly gets brighter
And brighter
The sound of children coming
Like the sound of drumming
Here they come
Round the corner
the sun as hot as a sauna
Carrying their school bags
And wearing their blazers
They arrive as sharp as razors
The girls scream and shout
About Blind Date last night
And the boys laugh and joke
About the fight
In they come running to the reg
Some boy jumping over a hedge
They go and see their teachers
'Today class, we are talking about preachers.'

Joe Gooden (14)
Hassenbrook School

SHOES

Red shoes, blue shoes
Old shoes, new shoes
Shoes that are black
Shoes that are white
Shoes that are loose
Shoes that are tight
Shoes with buckles
Shoes with bows
Shows that are narrow
and pinch your toes.

Shoes that are yellow
Shoes that are green
Shoes that are dirty
Shoes that are clean
Shoes for cold weather
Shoes for when it's hot
Shoes with laces
that get tangled in a knot.

David Walker (12)
Hassenbrook School

HOLIDAYS

Holidays - always great fun,
and then something goes terribly wrong,
you scrimp and save through all the week
and then suddenly the sink goes and leaks.

Holidays - can also be bad,
you queue up for a month, you queue up for a day,
you queue up on this, then you queue up for that,
you can queue up through April, you can queue up through May.

Roller-coasters, water flumes,
merry-go-rounds too,
go on a roller-coaster
it will make you feel blue.

Holiday's great
Holiday's fun,
unless you're prepared
never go on one.

Sam Spooner (11)
Hassenbrook School

LADY DIANA

She thought of other people before herself,
She helped the starving who live in the third world,
She was marvellous to everyone and everything she saw,
including the poor.

She was taken from us with a tragedy,
Which was never meant to be,
It hit us in the heart,
like a turning key.

We feel sorry for her family,
Including her boys,
They were very close to her,
and shared the same joys.

Her final resting place
Is in the middle of a lake,
Surrounded by flowers,
she has no heartache.

Lisa Orton (15)
Hassenbrook School

Spider In The Bath

There is a spider who lives under the bath.
He always takes the usual path,
Through the plug hole, up the chain,
Then he goes back down again.

He sits on the bath, admiring the view,
And then he suddenly sees you
And runs down the bath as fast as he can
And says, 'Who is that ugly man?'

Then you see the spider and turn on the tap,
You turn away and put your head in your lap,
I have to save him before he gets washed away
So now he lives for another day.

Just remember when you go to the loo
That spiders are more scared of you.

Lee Greaves (12)
Hassenbrook School

The Flood Of Death

Dark skies, gloomy, miserable and dull,
The world peaceful,
Suddenly *crash!*
Rain comes pounding down,
Water cascades, invading homes,
The wind begins to moan,
Flashes of lightning fill the sky,
Water spreading, cars floating,
Sound of rain hitting roofs,
Damaging everything in its sight,
All of a sudden it's . . . *over!*

Sophie Merrington (12)
Hassenbrook School

MY LOVE FOR YOU

Your face is sculpted
On my mind and heart,
I felt we had something
Right from the start.

But I let all that go,
I treated you bad,
I never thought
I'd feel this sad.

I believed in my heart,
That you were the one,
I thought we'd never part,
That we'd go on and on.

I wish I could turn back
The hands of time,
I could correct those mistakes,
Though I'm not sure I can.

Would it be different?
Would things turn out right?
I'll never know now,
You're out of my sight.

I can't say it to your face,
I know I'd cry,
But I will love you
Until the day I die.

Claire Girling (15)
Hassenbrook School

THE HORSE

It runs through the field,
As the wind sweeps its hair,
It flies like a whirlwind,
Without any care.

Its eyes wide and voluptuous,
Its skin black as coal,
Its personality so wild,
Its spirit, as free as its soul.

Its posture unique,
It's graceful and proud,
It gallops, says nothing,
Yet this seems so loud.

It processes a power,
So powerful, so strong,
But it stands there, stays quiet,
The silence so long . . .

Sarah Bates (16)
Hassenbrook School

WALES: THE WORLD OF MAGIC

The world of Wales looks like magic
Many have died there, it is so tragic.
Every time I'm there on my hols
Every time I'm there I think of trolls.

The world of Wales is full of goblins
They laugh at us when we're hobblin'
Every time we drive around
My heart starts to really pound.

The world of Wales is really great
People that live there are all your mate.
Always respect it
And never neglect it.

Thomas Fall (11)
Hassenbrook School

HALLOWE'EN

Tonight, because it was Hallowe'en,
I painted my face yellow and green.
I put on a witch's hat
And called to Flopsy, my black cat.
My eyes were black with mum's eye pencil,
I made some dangley spiders with my brother's stencil.
I put on my nails and my green false teeth,
I looked in the mirror and felt quite pleased.
I walked down the road looking for ghosts,
And nearly walked into a lamp post.
Everybody looked at me,
I must have been a sight to see.
I knocked at some doors and said 'Trick or treat,'
Some didn't answer, oh what a cheek.
Now I have had my bath and washed myself clean,
I'm going to bed to have a dream,
But I'm not going to dream about Hallowe'en.

Brooke Shelton (12)
Hassenbrook School

TOURISTS

Litter, litter, that's what they drop
then they walk into the distance
and start drinking some pop

Tourists can be good
They can be bad

One after another they all queue up
waiting to get in
to the Hard Rock Cafe

Tourists can be good
They can be bad

The French are disgusting
they all eat frogs
The Dutch stand around banging their clogs

Tourists can be good
They can be bad

They all stand around Trafalgar Square
It just seems to be their little lair

Tourists can be good
They can be bad

London, London that's where they group
standing around trying to make friends

Tourists can be good
They can be bad

The moral of this story is
don't hang around with tourists
they make you look bad.

Tourists can be good
but they're mostly *bad!*

Reiss Ellingford (11)
Hassenbrook School

MY NETBALL MATCH

The match had started
The whistle blew
From our positions out we flew

The ball was tossed up and down
The players started to run around

The ball was thrown into the net
One goal scored
Time for more yet

'Over here!' the Centre cried
But missed the ball - it went off-side

We battled on long and harsh
Up and down the court we passed
We did all that had to be done
And in the end our side *won!*

Abby Coote (13)
Hassenbrook School

MY FRIEND

Me and my mates hang around,
Up the park and up the town.
One of my mates,
Moved away,
Now I'm scared
I'll never see her again.

She was the best,
Better than the rest.
It was a shame,
That she moved away,
Because I'm scared
I'll never see her again.

Claire Burgess (11)
Hassenbrook School

LOVE

Put aching legs
On a soft chair
Cheek flattened against
The cold window
Watch lights dance outside
From the speeding night train
Doze to the rhythm
Reach your stop
Wish you could stay
There
Forever.

Katie Bird (16)
Havering Sixth Form College

DOLPHINS

Dolphins, dolphins everywhere,
Swimming around like they don't care.
Jumping out of the water,
Swimming free.

Swimming so fast,
Catching fish,
Minding their own business.
Ever so friendly,
Also cuddly.

Swim with them,
Play with them,
They don't mind,
As long as you treat them kind.

Samantha Brimfield (12)
King Edmund School

MEN!

Most men they can be slobs,
Most men are quite crazy,
Most men are big fat blobs,
All men are always lazy.

All men love some sort of sport,
Most men either drink or smoke,
Some men may be quite short,
But love them or not they're all just blokes.

Emma Flaherty (12)
King Edmund School

School Time

I have to get up early, to go to my new school.
On Mondays it's assembly taken in the hall.
On Tuesdays it's PE, a sport for every taste.
But alas in tales of woe some can't stand the pace.

There are lots of different subjects on the timetable.
On Wednesdays it is drama, the stage is set for all.
On Thursdays it is art, we hope to be inspired.
With our brush and paint on fire.

On Fridays it's technology, to the kitchen we must go.
With a mixture of ingredients we end up with a dough.
In the oven with our mixture which soon begins to rise.
Hopefully in thirty minutes out will come our pies.

Karlie Mason (11)
King Edmund School

Without You . . .

Without you the world would have no colour.
Without you I would not be me.
Without you there would be no heaven.
Without you my heart would never beat.
Without you the wheels of life wouldn't turn.
Without you Cupid's arrow wouldn't strike.
Without you my blood would run cold.
Without you the world would stop forever!

Emily-Jane Betsworth (12)
King Edmund School

TORTOISE

With the hard shell shining green
With the green legs slowly moving
With the red tongue flicking out
With the eyes flashing.

Eating salad
Lettuce and cabbage
Tomatoes and cucumber
And potatoes on the side.

Walking around in my garden
Over the grass and
Under the trees
Waiting for me to come home.

In the winter
In the box
Hibernating
Fast asleep.

Brett O'Donnell (11)
King Edmund School

TITANIC

As you saw a ship rise gracefully
and take its last breath of air,
as it fell to its bed of coral,
the same happened to a newborn baby
as its mother slowly passed
whilst holding it in the icy cold water,
it took its last breath and slowly looked around,
as if to say *why!*

Stacey Edwards (11)
King Edmund School

SEASONS

Spring is colourful,
Bulbs split open up come flowers,
Houses get spring cleaned.

Summer is yellow,
Hot and sticky,
Paddling pools all come out.

Autumn is brown,
Covered in leaves,
The time when bin bags are all used up.

Winter is white,
Wet and cold,
The season I like most.

Matthew Gray (12)
King Edmund School

SPORT

Sports are fun for you to play
There's lots of rules you must obey.
Start with football and have some fun
And hope your team's the winning one.
Now try tennis and stretch your legs
Hit the ball and not your head.
What about hockey? That sure is fun
It gives good exercise for everyone.
Now join a team, whatever you play
And enjoy yourself on a sports day.

Rachel Maddocks (11)
King Edmund School

IN THE JUNGLE

In the jungle you will find
cheeky monkeys swing
from vine to vine
elephants stomping round.

In the jungle you will find
pandas quiet as night
so black and white
snakes so shiny silvery green.

In the jungle you will find
tigers flaming orange eyes
lions running roaring sound
echoing in the jungle around.

Stephanie Ballinger (11)
King Edmund School

WILD ANIMALS

The fiery tiger with colours so bright
A brown hairy monkey makes noises at night

A big grey elephant stomping around
He likes his nuts so crispy and brown

A sad white panda with no more bamboo
Down came the rain and it just grew and grew and grew.

Joanna Wells (11)
King Edmund School

ICE HEART

It was there
By the door
But she's been there before
It was there by the door
It is broken now.

It was there
By the door
She looked as before
There by the door
It proclaimed.

Dark shadows formed
Though she felt warm
The reaper fools
The heart is cooled
It is broken now.

Stand by the door
It is there evermore
Is it a law
To be known?
The heart is alone.

Joanne Hilbery (15)
King Edmund School

DINNER WITH MY LITTLE BROTHER

I have a little brother, he likes to eat toast
He flicks it up and down and dips it in his roast
He put it in the video, he leaves it in the bath
Mum gets very angry, he thinks it's just a laugh.

Marc Ely (11)
King Edmund School

ODE TO LEAH KEY

Whenever I'm in times of need,
and want to pine away,
I can always rely on my best friend,
to help and comfort me.
We've known each other since we were small,
though time hasn't flown at all.
You make me laugh,
you make me smile,
with all your jokes and silly giggle.
Your stories are rubbish,
but still we laugh,
the times we've had have been such a blast.
You've had bad times,
and so have I,
we've always had a shoulder on which we can cry,
I know on you I can rely.
To my best pal Leah Key,
our friendship shall never expire.
I hope that we are friends for life,
until we both die.

Donna Cattell (15)
King Edmund School

FIRE

The crackling of the flames,
heat pouring off, people sitting
in front of it warming themselves up,
smoke drifting away
up, up into the air,
far, far away.

Ashley North (11)
King Edmund School

My Pets

My pets, I have five,
four girls and one boy
and they all live outside in a hutch.

They're all different colours,
and all different sizes,
and it's true that they eat like a pig.

One mum and three babies,
all grey and white,
and not forgetting Snowy
who squeaks all night.

When they're in the run,
they hide in the tunnel,
and never want to come out.

Samantha Elbra (11)
King Edmund School

When My Cat Died

When my cat died I cried and cried
I knew that I would miss him
He was a soft and fluffy cat
But a little dim.
He used to sit and watch the birds
For hours at a time
And often trotted down the garden
To look for a tree to climb.

Neil Whitehead (11)
King Edmund School

MY DOG

Snores loudly in his bed
Walks slowly on four legs
But runs as fast as lightning
Sometimes he's so exciting.

Good at catching bouncy balls
Excellent at jumping over walls
Always happy to go to the park
Will hop into bed when it gets dark.

Eats quickly off his plate
But never puts on weight
Likes a stretch in the morning
You can always hear him yawning.

I would never give him away,
Even though he barks all day.
My dog, he's so great
That's why he's my best mate!

Laurie Hetherington (12)
King Edmund School

FIRE

Bang, spit, crackle, went the fire,
It's orangey-red that it is.
Its hot fire flames are like a dragon
With its head held high
All the children at the fence looking at my
Fire flame dragon.

Clare Sloan (11)
King Edmund School

MY SCHOOL BAG

In my school bag things hide away,
like mouldy old sandwiches that have gone grey.

My school books are covered in drink and slime.
My friend said to me 'That's just like mine.'

I opened a compartment and there I saw
My smelly PE socks, everyone said *'Phoar!'*

My pens and pencils are scattered everywhere.
I can't find my Parker, oh look, it's there!

Well now you know what I hide away.
Don't tell anyone, it's a secret, OK?

Zoe Young (11)
King Edmund School

HORROR

A spooky castle just sitting on the moor,
I walked up to the battered old door.
I rang the bell but no reply.
Then all of a sudden the door opens wide.
Scary noises, horrible smells fly around,
Up and down ghosts fly all night long.
All of a sudden I see something
What is it? A headless man, oh no!
I ran and ran through the battered door
Across the spooky graveyard,
Through the old gates across the moor
And home I am

I never want to know again!

Emma Pickrell (11)
King Edmund School

BLOOD ON THE WAR FIELD

Armies of British soldiers,
Ready to fight for their country,
As they step on the battlefield,
Courageous and brave soldiers ready to fight.
Heavy noises of gunshot run through the night.
After a hard and courageous night,
Morning finally comes.
Women and children wake
To find a letter on their doorstep
To say why their fathers, brothers, sons, did not come home.

Families mourn over dead bodies.
The battlefield is now silent,
While the country has victory
For the soldiers that gave up their lives
To save others.

Kirsty Rustman (11)
King Edmund School

ANIMALS IN THE WILD

A stripy tiger with colours so bright
A cobra hunting for food at night
A mosquito gives a nasty bite
A barn owl with such a wonderful sight
A robin glides like a kite
A crocodile suddenly strikes

Laura Hessey (12)
King Edmund School

MY PET MOUSE

His favourite hobby is to play,
He runs around his cage all day,
And even when we are in bed,
He never seems to rest his head.

He's got a tube, a house, a nest,
But he seems to like his wheel the best,
You would think that he'd get dizzy,
For a mouse who is so 'diddy'.

He eats some food,
And drinks some drink,
He's got brown hair,
But he really does stink!

I get him out all the time,
I'm very proud that he's mine,
He's the best at acrobatics,
He can make himself as flat as flat.

Kirsty Morgan (12)
King Edmund School

CREEPY CASTLES

Creepy castles are scary
Creepy castles are frightening
The stairs creek
The ghosts peep
The castles are so big you will get lost
If you get lost you will pay the cost.

Do not enter creepy castles.

Ashley Wallace-Merrett (11)
King Edmund School

MIGHTY MARS - GOD OF WAR

Marching loudly into action
Armour shining, blinding
Ready to kill is *Mars!*
Swords swing, swung - blood gushes.

Gods - *boom, crash, wallop!*
Over the sea of fighting soldiers
Dying warriors

Out came his shiny mighty sword
Fierce gods wanting to win

War ends with a scattered army
At last the gods are destroyed
Romans are victorious.

Marcus Sowerbutts (13)
King Edmund School

FOOD

I am hungry, I want some food!
To fill my tummy, to make it huge.
Mouldy or not, give it to me
'Cause I really don't care,
Just please, please, please, give me my tea.
My favourite food just has to be,
A lump of cake and a cup of tea.
Well now you know what I have for a feast,
Now just go away, you horrible beast.

Laura Dinning (12)
King Edmund School

A WINTER'S DREAM

Winter's coming, everything's cold
Freezing frosty ice poles,
Chucked away from the summer.
The children give a large murmur.
Go outside, see the snow, run about.
Feet are cold.
Snowballs flying like World War II
Children screaming, faces blue.
Sledges going up and down,
Children slipping on the ground.
Madness is everywhere.
Old people in wheelchairs.
Skating round on the pond.
Grannies screaming.
Grandads daydreaming.
It's a winter's dream come true.

Rachel Barrass (13)
King Edmund School

HALLOWE'EN

It is the 31st. It's Hallowe'en.
Pumpkins are everywhere to be seen.
Blood and gory bits,
Head teachers having fits.
Out of the graveyard come zombies,
Scary monsters with fleas,
Vampires and witches are lurking about,
But worst of all there are
    Brussels sprouts!

Jordan Pillai (11)
King Edmund School

LONELY HEART

A fine friendly lady I'm looking to meet
To make my Christmas swing
Someone to spark my youthful streak
And treat me like a king.
So stop me feeling alone
And make my Christmas dream
Stop my waiting by the phone
And let my sad eyes gleam.
So do be a gem, and answer this ad
By phone or with a letter
Stop me feeling down and sad
Because with you Christmas seems much better.
Ohh! Is that the phone that I can hear?
Saturday night? Of course my dear!

Erin Smith (12)
King Edmund School

WAR

War is ferocious,
War is disastrous,
Bloody ground,
With people bound
To get killed.
Bombs are falling like rain,
As people are crying in pain.
Jet planes flying overhead
As people mourn for their dead.
All war zones are dangerous,
With soldiers all around us.

Ciaran O'Shaughnessy (11)
King Edmund School

KATIE LONDESBOROUGH

My friend is Katie Londesborough,
and Anne Marie too, but Katie's
always there for me, when I'm feeling blue.

My friend is Katie Londesborough,
she's always there to help,
Her hair is brown, she has sparkling eyes.

My friend is Katie Londesborough
whenever in doubt, she's always about
to help who she can and please everyone.

My friend isn't Katie Londesborough
as we had a fight.
I wish we didn't have one now
as I'm on my own.
She's sitting in the other room
without a doubt in mind.
My friend was Katie Londesborough
                    but now it's just to spite.

Lauren Button (13)
King Edmund School

COUNTRYSIDE

Sun, sun, in the sky
Birds flying on the mountainside.
Corn cut fresh, clean and spiky on the ground.
A scarecrow standing, straw sticking out,
Ragged clothes, torn and battered.
A pheasant walking, barely making a sound,
Pretty and elegant colour on its tail,
Like a rainbow.

Laura Vickery (11)
King Edmund School

CLUELESS

Clueless underneath
Lifeless on outside
Ugly as she seems
Every beauty hides
Love and happiness
Everyone can see
She is very special
Special to me.

Clueless underneath
Underneath she sighs
Sighs with relief
Relief in her eyes
Eyes are rich and blue
Blue is dark and frail
Frail is her all over
Over is the tale.

Rachael Clifford (12)
King Edmund School

WINTER

Winter is coming
Put on your coat,
Get ready for hibernation,
While we go on a vacation
To a hot and sunny island
While you are freezing.
Sleeping, sleeping,
Till eventually
Summer comes again.

Andrew Loughlin (11)
King Edmund School

DREAMS AND NIGHTMARES!

Some people say that if you watch a horror movie late at night,
that you'll never know what could give you such a fright.
But when I watch a scary film before I go to bed,
I always end up with a bump on the head
rolling from side to side, falling out of my bed.

Some people sleepwalk and some people snore
but the really odd thing is that you can never remember what your
nightmare was about,
the harder you think, the more it's gone,
the less you think the more it's there.
So how come you never forget the word 'nightmare'
but you always forget your nightmares.

A nightmare could be frightening, or it could be sad,
A nightmare you can't remember when you wake up you think
you're mad.
So never look forward to a dream or nightmare, 'cause when you
wake up, you never know what they're about!

Waisan Lee (13)
King Edmund School

AUTUMN

Leaves, leaves on the ground,
Gentle breeze rushing through my hair,
The trees are whistling,
I love playing with the leaves,
Climbing the trees,
Higher and higher,
I love autumn and autumn loves me.

Amy Burrows (12)
King Edmund School

What A Mess!

Clothes on the carpet,
Pens on the floor,
Bought from the market,
Don't want them anymore.
It's time for bed,
But it's still in a heap,
I flop down dead,
And try to sleep.
New Year's resolution,
To keep this room tidy,
Is this the solution?
Won't last till Friday.
Next year I'll try again,
By then Mum will be insane!

Katie Garner (12)
King Edmund School

Waiting For The Morning To Come

Stars shining like the morning sun
The mist gleaming over the houses
The dew settling in the grass
And the moon reflecting in the icy ponds and lakes
Waiting for the morning to come.
At last the morning comes
The cold winter day begins
And the sound of happiness in the air
As children play in the snow.

David Matthews Fahr (12)
King Edmund School

MY HOLIDAY IN FLORIDA

I wake up to the boiling sun
It looks like a golden golf ball hit from far away,
I get dressed into my blue bikini
Then stroll along the white beach,
After, I walk to the shiny pool.

Splash! The cold water smacks my face.
The relaxing water cools me down,
I get out and walk to the beach.
I lay out my towel and lie on it,
I fall asleep with the sun blazing in my face
And the palm trees swaying with the gentle breeze.

Then suddenly I wake, my feet are cold,
I look down and the sea has come right up to me.
I look at my watch and it's lunchtime,
I get up and go to lunch, I buy a fruit bowl,
I put a piece of pineapple in my mouth, *hmm!* So juicy!

After that with my mouth refreshed,
I go back to my house and get dressed.

Natasha Child (12)
King Edmund School

STORM

I watched the sky as it turned black,
The lightning bolted and then flashed,
The clouds rumbled by heavy with their load,
Of pure white rain, ready to dispose.

It fell from the heavens, high above,
Relentlessly pouring like streams of doves,
I watched it from my cosy room,
The thunder went on like impending doom.

Puddles formed, rivers swelled,
It even filled up the old wishing well,
I got up at that and grabbed my coat and my hat,
I went out and braved the storm and felt a new dawn.

A new dawn approached over the hill,
I ran out to it, with time to kill,
I watched it rise, I felt its warmth,
The storm was now out, I felt reborn.

Emily Whistler (15)
King Edmund School

LEAVING

As I sat at home,
As I lay on my bed,
I had many different thoughts
running through my head.
Why did that happen? What did I do?
Then I sat up as I thought of you.
How you cheered me up when I was blue,
you made me laugh, you made me live.
When I think of what you made me give,
I want you back.
I need to see your face again,
I need something to ease the pain.
Why did you leave, where did you go?
What is going to happen? I don't really know.
I lay back down with tears in my eyes,
All I need to do is cry.
As I think of all the pain you've caused,
I feel as if my life has paused.

Emma Bale (16)
King Edmund School

THE SNOW

Fluffy and white like a blanket,
Covering the land as far as I can see,
It shines and glistens in the light,
Like soft cotton wool sparkling in the sun.

Crunchy as I step on it,
And cold when I feel it,
Snow makes everything look clean,
It brightens up the land as far as I can see.

Roofs are covered and gardens too,
Footprints making patterns,
And children having fun,
Throwing snowballs,
Building snowmen,
But then out comes the sun.

In no time at all,
What was once clean and white,
Has turned slushy and slippery, slidey and wet.
People no longer playing or having fun,
But staying behind closed doors
Now the snow has gone.

Emma Liddell (12)
King Edmund School

THE SEABED

Down in the bottom of the seabed,
with brown and yellow sand,
there lies a cockle shell.
In that cockle shell there lies a shiny pearl,
lying in the seabed all shimmering with green.

Karina Irlam (12)
King Edmund School

118

THE NIGHT

The moon shines brightly,
Her pale shimmering light
Softly coating the cool darkness of the night
Calming the world and the people.

The fox hunts, scavenging for food
In dustbins and around the streets he looks,
While the hedgehog slowly saunters through a garden
On a midnight ramble.

A small distance away,
The nightly traffic rumbles on.
But a lone cricket chirps while mice scurry around,
A tasty dinner for the now silent owl who watches carefully.

The night!
Dark and mystical, it soothes the sun-baked Earth,
The deepness makes it seem as if
The only person alive is you.

Suddenly, a crack of light appears.
A sunray shoots up, cracking the blackness.
The day is nearly here and the night must go -
Until tomorrow's night.

Danielle Levett (12)
King Edmund School

THE PARTY

We're having a party today
We've invited a lot of people.
Here they come.
The cars are drawing up. *Vroom, screech!*
Ringing the doorbells. *Buzz, ding, ding.*
Time for a little dance. *Tap, tap, boom, boom, tra-la-la!*
Time for some food. *Scoff, scoff, scoff.*
Bit of annoyance. *Aaah!* Flying plate.
Oh no, here's a food fight. *Crash, bang, smash, splat, crack!*
Oh dear. Now they've started a proper fight. *Oof, smash, whack, clonk!*
Here come the police. *Nee-nah, nee-nah, nee-nah!*
Oops, everyone's going. *Screech, vroom.*
Oops, you'd better make an emergency stop. *Bang!*
Oh - too late! Ambulance coming. *Nee-naw, nee-naw, nee-naw.*
Now ambulance is leaving. *Nee-naw, nee-naw, nee-naw.*
Miaow!
Oh dear, the neighbours are complaining about their cat.

Moan, groan, mutter.

A fight ensues. *Smash, whack, pow, smack.*
The police are coming again. *Nee-nah, nee-nah, nee-nah.*

Here we go again!

Ben Goldstein (12)
King Edmund School

FLYING HIGH

I was sitting in an aeroplane,
we were flying high.
Then we started to go down,
falling from the sky.
I shouted 'Help!' but no-one came
Just as I ran out of hope,
a kind of bird came flying by.
'Jump on me and we shall fly,'
I jumped on his little back.
'Close your eyes' he said,
1, 2, 3, I opened my eyes.
Wasn't I shocked to see
the four walls of a room
everywhere around me!

Liane Thomas (13)
King Edmund School

RABBIT

The grey furry rabbit likes hopping
quickly and running fast.
He jumps into a field of juicy carrots
and green grass.
He chews and chews and chews all day and
then he likes to run and play.
His fur is grey, the grass is green.
The rabbit is the best you've seen,.
His ears are long, his teeth are strong,
When you're with Rabbit, you can't go wrong.

Gemma Butcher (13)
King Edmund School

THE BEACH

The beach is a wonderful place
The sea is deep and blue
The sand is golden and warm
I think you'll like it too.
Go down to the shore in your cossies
Let the water grab your feet
Run right through the breakers
Say 'Hi' to the creatures you meet
The starfish will give you a wave
No doubt the sea will too
The crabs will give you a friendly nip
You can try and give them a pinch too
Watch out for the jellyfish
They might give you a sting
But don't worry too much,
It's just a friendly thing!

Andrea Place (12)
King Edmund School

PERFORMING

Lights are dimming, spotlights on
The dancer is ready, excited in the wings
Music is beginning, get ready, get ready
Now . . .
Twirling gracefully across the stage
Skirts swirling and shimmering
Concentrate, remember the steps
Danced so many times before
Smile, smile, as the last step comes
Before I leave the stage.

Vivienne Stenhouse (12)
King Edmund School

ODE TO A SPECIAL FRIEND

Friends forever
Always together
Never to part
You'll break my heart
When I'm not with you
It makes me blue
Put bad times behind
Straight out of mind
Life's just begun
So let's have some fun
I hate to say goodbye
It usually makes me cry
So always be my friend
Together till the end.

Lisa Dabbs (16)
King Edmund School

SWIMMING

I gracefully dived into the pool,
Through the water I swam,
Lengths and lengths.
Front crawl,
Back crawl,
Breaststroke,
Splash!
People on the beach were soaked,
Slowly I crawled out the water,
My legs felt like wobbling orange jelly,
I grabbed my towel and went for a shower.

Natalie Hayward (12)
King Edmund School

HIDDEN DEPTHS

Look into the light and you'll see only darkness,
Gaze into the unknown and you'll see only me.
The gap between hunter and prey is decreasing;
Look behind you and the angels don't sing.

I am immortal and your soul is mine:
Watching the waves of sand falling through time.
To be part of a world so evil and true,
Is what I'll give if I fall for you.

To form and to love are two different things,
To save and to live are not joined.
But to live and give life are two of the same -
I'll be your life, your love and I'll own your name.

Words are lies and lies are love;
I'm a forgotten menace brought down from above.
I am black, no longer the wings of your dove;
For my words are lies and your words are love.

I'd cross the ocean and waves of blue
If required, to come and see you.
For you, my love, I need a cure -
Your blood, my love, so sweet and pure.

Sarah Anne Brown (15)
King Edmund School

A Holiday In The Caribbean

I wake up in the morning to the boiling ball of sun.
It looks gorgeous outside with the palm trees
blowing lightly in the breeze.
I decide to get dressed into my bathing suit
and lay under the palm trees with the sun
shining down on me.

I woke up to the sound of the relaxing waves
and I decide to get up, and a delicious cocktail
was ready and waiting.
My feet were sinking into the fine sand,
it made me want to dive into the swimming pool
so I could cool down.

I fell asleep on a lilo in the pool so long that
the blazing sun gave me a tan.
After that beautiful sleep I went for a stroll.

It was so peaceful and quiet,
so I walked down to the cafe and bought
a drink to take up to my hotel.
After a long day I threw myself on the bed
and fell fast asleep.
It became night-time so soon and I
wasn't tired any more, so I went outside,
sat on the beach and gazed up at the stars.

Joanna Cross (12)
King Edmund School

JOVI

There he stood, grazing alone,
I wonder if he knew this was his new home,
I had waited for this moment as never before,
My very own horse, I wanted no more.

My mind began to race,
Of the moments we would share,
We would ride together as one,
Over the hills without a care.

The wind rushing at my face,
Trying to hold us back,
Branches snatching in front of our eyes,
As we raced along the track.

His elegant legs,
Lengthening with each stride,
The power they possessed,
No fear did he hide.

Together at last,
Never to part,
We will ride as one,
As one, from the heart.

Bonnie Young (16)
King Edmund School

THE TEDDY BEAR

Creeping up the stairs
and heading for my bed
is my favourite pussy cat
my fluffy 'Mr Ted'.

He sneaks really quietly
until he's next to me
then he makes lots of noise
while purring loudly.

He lays with me
until early morning
when I'm awake
and yawning.

I love my cat
he's nice to me
he's my best friend
the best he can be!

Danielle Jones (12)
King Edmund School

FRIENDS

We have been friends for many years,
It's always your innocent voice I hear.
If we were ever parted, I would shed a tear,
The ending of our friendship is my only fear.
So please listen to me now
So I can make my feelings clear,
Your friendship means the world to me
So always be close and near.

Louise Simpson (16)
King Edmund School

MY PETS

Kitty's my cat with biscuit coloured fur,
It likes to purr,
He prowls along the road,
Miaowing as he goes.

Sparkle's my dog,
With its black and white fur,
If I'm holding a bone,
Then she won't go far.

Ben's my other dog,
With his black and brown fur,
He likes to roll around,
Acting the clown.

Laura Dobson (11)
King Edmund School

PARTING

10 years since our friendship started,
Only another year till we're parted.
Following our own dreams and careers,
Sharing our thoughts and our fears.
Together through sadness and pain,
Walking home through thunder and rain.
Forward into a new beginning,
So we can begin living.
Life has only just begun,
So remember to be happy and have fun.

Lisa Stanley (16)
King Edmund School

TIGER, TIGER

Tiger, tiger running wild
Stripy back and a big, long tail
Big ears and whiskers too
Sitting there looks at you

Tiger, tiger running wild
Jumping, pouncing, roaring loud
Purring softly as he sleeps
Licking his chops for tasty meat

Tiger, tiger running wild
Getting sleepy as sun goes down
Walking back to its humble home
Tiger, tiger don't go now.

Amy Thomas (11)
King Edmund School

THE MIDNIGHT FOX

The midnight fox enters the forest.
I hear leaves rustling.
The cold breeze rushing through my hair.
I see the fox and the fox sees me.
Its cold nose touches my cold fingers.
The fox takes a step backwards.
The fox runs into his cold, dark hideout.
I walk back into the wood trying to find my way back.
The wind is cold, I'm all alone.

Charlotte Witchell (12)
King Edmund School

DOLPHINS

Dolphins like to swim
Through the waves
Jumping up high
Playing with their babies
Looking for food to feed on.

Dolphins are trained
So that they can do shows
Where people stand and cheer
And watch what they do
After the show the dolphins get fed.

And then they are put to bed
In the morning they get up
They eat their breakfast
Then they are ready
For another long day.

Leanne Gray (11)
King Edmund School

THE PITCH

One stormy night on a wet football pitch,
Teams did battle to see who were the best.
Goals in their minds, trophies in their dreams,
The fans shout their teams' nicknames - Devils, Gunners.
But only one team emerges victorious,
Some fans with joy, some with sorrow.
And so the stadium is silent,
Till the next time those twenty-two players
Run out on that pitch.

Danny Bridge (12)
King Edmund School

PENNY

Black as midnight
Loud as thunder
Loves to play and fight
Licks me with her slimy tongue.

Penny is the name of my dog
Understands every word I say
Then rolls over and acts like a log
I say speak and then a woof! . . . rings the bell.

It's time to go to sleep now Penny
She sobs and goes in her basket
Don't cry I say I will see you tomorrow
Too late she's already gone off.

Jenna Harrington (11)
King Edmund School

SUMMER

Walking along the beach,
The sun is high out of reach,
The blue sky is very bright,
With not a cloud in sight,
Yellow sand hot with the sun's heat,
Waves splashing against my feet,
People lying on the sand,
Getting very burned and tanned,
Some children playing with a frisbee,
Splashing and jumping in the sea,
Everybody eating ice-cream,
Oh well, it was all a dream!

Toni Clarke (13)
King Edmund School

My Horse

As I sit upon my horse,
I gaze at its shiny coat,
its flaxen mane and doe like eyes,
that horse I love the most.
It whinnies at me lovingly
when I come to call,
together we canter across the fields,
with not a care in the world.
My horse and I were best friends,
until that fateful day.
I pushed open the stable door
and on the floor he lay.
He did not stir, he did not breathe,
looked like he was asleep,
but yet he had slipped into
an everlasting sleep.

Carlie Page (13)
King Edmund School

The Haunted House

The children entered the haunted house,
Creeping around as silent as a mouse.
Looking for the ghastly ghost,
Which is talked about the most.
Making their way through room by room,
Suddenly the ghost appeared from the gloom.
The children froze like ice on the floor,
And then they fled through the door.
They ran all the way home.

Emma Cotgrove (13)
King Edmund School

EARLY START!

I wake up at dawn,
Normally with a yawn,
I look at the clock,
And it says 6 o'clock,
Quiet and still I lay,
Wishing I could sleep all day,
It's not long before I hear a shout,
It's my mum saying time to get out,
I get up all sleepy eyed,
But all is not lost,
My eggs are fried,
I eat my eggs and drink my tea,
Then look in the mirror,
And yes it's me!

Paul Pedder (14)
King Edmund School

MY SISTER

I had a young sister Siobhan
She died when only eight hours old
I could not stop crying whilst
She was dying, but she was gone.

The day she died I cried and cried
I just couldn't help it
I never even saw her
Only in a picture.

Chris Duffy (13)
King Edmund School

THE KEY

Where is the key
That opens his heart?
Why doesn't it open?
Why don't the doors part?

Where is the key
That opens the lock?
What must I do
To get past this great block?

How can I please him
By being myself?
Maybe I'll leave him
Alone with his wealth.

I wait until morning
Then we will part,
Because I can't find the key
That opens his heart.

Hannah Prince (13)
King Edmund School

MISSING YOU!

It seems like only yesterday you were here,
but now you've gone and nowhere near.
I think of you but it brings a tear,
onto my cheek then down to my ear.
I lay in bed silently weeping,
when people see me composure keeping.
Hours later I end up sleeping,
I miss you so much,
we mustn't lose touch.

Natalie Smith (15)
King Edmund School

SUMMER FUN

Green, green grass
The sun as bold as brass
High in the sky
Shining brightly in my eye
Flowers gently winking in the sun
Kids laughing and having fun
School is out
Kids scream and shout
They're free at last
White fluffy clouds above
This is the season that I love
The fresh warm air
Gently blowing through my hair
Blowing trees
In the breeze
It's a lovely sunny day.

Laura Kenton (13)
King Edmund School

NO

I met a girl as peaceful as a dove
You know I think I might be in love
With eyes as blue as the sea
I really hope she likes me
She has long flowing locks
So what if she smells of old socks
I can't decide if to ask the girl
Perhaps I should get her a ring, with a pearl
I finally decide to ask her out
Only to hear her shout.
No!

Mike Thorpe (13)
King Edmund School

LIVING WITHOUT YOU

I don't know why you did that,
Left me all alone,
I don't know why I love you still,
I guess I'll never know.
But I can't stop thinking about you
And the way we used to be,
I can't understand why you did this,
Why did it have to be me?

I sit here alone,
Wondering what to do,
I can't believe I'm here
Living without you.
My life is full of sadness,
Love was just a game,
Without you in my life,
I will never be the same.

I thought love was forever,
All love and happiness,
Instead it's a disaster,
All full of tearfulness.
Marriage and devotion,
Was what I was hoping for,
I can't believe you left me
As now I want you more.

I can't believe this sorrow,
All the heartbreak and pain,
It's like living in hell,
Never seeing you again.
I wake up every morning,
Wondering what to do,
I know what I want in my life now,
What I want is you.

Louise Naylor (16)
King Edmund School

A SUMMER'S DAY

As the birds floated across the
                    clear, blue sky,
And I thought to myself how quickly
                    winter has passed by,
The grass felt warm like a winter's
                    log fire,
As I lay there thinking of my long
                    heart's desire.
It all went silent, not a sound
                    for miles.
'Plonk' a little duckling went as it looked
                    as if it was in the swimming trials.
The soft breeze just caught the end
                    of my hair,
As I could smell the sweet
                    country air.
The time was ticking, ticking,
                    ticking away.
But there was nothing bad to think
                    about on this hot summer's day.

Samantha Neary (13)
King Edmund School

MISGUIDED FANTASIES

The first night I saw you,
And our eyes met,
You were the blonde, cute one,
I was the brunette.

It felt like a dream,
It could have been fate,
The way we were,
On our very first date.

It was a great romance,
But it didn't last long,
I thought it was forever,
But then it was gone.

The last time I saw you,
That night in the pool,
We were having such fun,
Acting the fool.

We were so stupid,
So unprepared,
Why did you do it?
For a bet, a dare?

You know we were careless,
We acted like fools,
Now you've gone and left me,
With troubles and all.

Helen Davis (15)
King Edmund School

DREAMS

In my dreams I'm taken to Fantasy World,
Where dragons, the colour of sunlit skies,
Clash in the afterworld.
They roar with wrath and squeal with fright to rise
Above each other.

Magic only exists in dreamland,
Where wizards read from dusty spellbound parchments.
They quarrel over curses, and
Practice sorcery to see whom is the most prevalent.

In underworld dark creatures lurk,
Underwater in the depths of the ocean,
Archeons and massive sharks,
Hide round mighty coral reefs.

Enchantress world is where fairies play,
In delves of pink and silver,
The other gremlins bicker all day
In a most taunting way.

In our own world,
All these things occur,
Whether it be in dreamland or underworld,
We must soon find a cure.

The battle between good and evil
Has gone on for a long time,
We have got to be fair,
And turn our world into a place of harmony.

Sarah Barker (13)
King Edmund School

LOVER'S TALE

My hatred for you
Grew and grew
You walked out of the door
And left me on my own.

It was over long ago
Memories of you long ago
Left in my torn mind.

You ripped me shred to shred
As you strike me with your head
I'm glad you are gone.

You put me through such cruelty
Treating me like a dog
You scarred my life forever
And now you're gone.

Admir Bajramoyic (13)
King Edmund School

FIRE

Fire is a red hot flame
like paint thrown against a wall
destructing everything in its path
with its distinctive crackling
and black smoke
expressing its anger
as if it had been disturbed
while it torments everything
in an upset mood
with an evil glow.

Tom Hale (13)
King Edmund School

LEAVING

Will you still be there when I get home?
Yesterday I was sure
But now I am not.
I recall the days you hurt me
When you bruised me black and blue
And wonder time and time again,
Do I want you back,
Back in my life when all you've done
Is cause me so much pain?
Will I miss you if you go?
How will I cope with life alone?
The only thing that I am sure of
Is that if you go I can heal
The wounds that you made.

Rachel Field (14)
King Edmund School

HALLOWE'EN

On the night of Hallowe'en
Everyone hides, trying not to be seen
Only children run around the street,
Knocking on doors calling 'Trick or treat'
If you refuse the treat, within the hour
You'll find your doorstep covered in flour!
Children parade, carrying pumpkins lit with candles
Witches supposedly fly on old broom handles
The children in their costume dress
Dancing and chanting with eeriness
All the children have fun and play
This is the eve of All Saint's Day.

Robert Reeves (14)
King Edmund School

A Sudden Shudder Of Fear

As I rested peacefully in my huge, snug four-poster bed,
I felt safe from my fears as if I was being cared for in my deep slumber.
Comfortably I felt cut off from the outside world as I fell dead,
As I counted in my drowse of many numbers.

However, a sudden light breeze fell across my nose,
Which caused me to wake from my sleep.
I shot up like a dart being thrown into a singe,
As the sudden shock made me begin to weep,
However, all that happened was my curtain flapping in the wind.

I arose from bed to secure the mysteriously opened vent,
Where I suppose the breeze must have come from the waters of Kent.

Verity Robinson (13)
King Edmund School

Words

Rude words sniff and pick their noses,
  Loving words clutch crimson roses,
    Hot words boil and bubble,
      Cold words shiver and huddle,
        Short words stand on their tiptoes,
          While tall words peer straight down their nose,
            Angry words stamp their feet and yell,
              Stubborn words like to repel,
                Lazy words lounge about,
                  Beautiful words always pout,
                  Swear words always scream and shout,
                Worried words are always in doubt,
              Giggling words are always laughing,
            Sharing words are forever halving.

Sarah Porter (14)
King Edmund School

HALLOWE'EN

I saw a black cat sat upon a fence
Its bottle-green eyes stood out
Against the dark night skies
It spied a mouse lurking about.

I felt the damp night air
It was close
There was something about tonight
That sent shivers down my spine.

I could hear rustling trees
That sounded like bees
Humming in the breeze
And small feet pattering along the ground.

Suddenly, from out of sight
A skeleton, a goblin, a ghost
Popped out, stranger than most
My heart beat with all its might.

There was something about tonight
That sent shivers down my spine
Like a thousand volts
Do you know why?

Because it's Hallowe'en night.

Parris Simmons (13)
King Edmund School

DOLPHIN WORLD

Deeper, deeper, deeper,
Down to the dolphin world.
What we'll find we do not know.
The pressure gets harder but we carry on
Until we hear the dolphin song.
Then slowly but surely from nose to tail
The dolphins appear with a flick and a wail.
With shiny bodies and big, black eyes
The dolphins swim with grace and poise.

As we follow the dolphins
We see how they play,
We see how they feed
And watch them all day.
They swim to the surface
Then dive round and round,
Towards the cold, sandy ground.

Soon we must leave them in their world,
Swirling and twirling until they feel the time has come
To say goodbye to everyone.

Alice Taylor (15)
King Edmund School

MY PET MOUSE

I have a pet mouse
He escaped in the house
We laid out a trap
Upon the front mat
As he ran up the hall
It looked ever so cool
He was really so nifty
And must have touched fifty.

He's not like any other
But he's got to go said my mother
So down went the cheese
Because I do aim to please
At last he was caught
Then I had a bright thought
If mice are forbidden
I must keep him hidden.

Leah Wright (11)
King Edmund School

HALLOWE'EN

Witches, witches everywhere,
Spotty skin and greasy hair,
Black, skinny, sneaky cats,
Slimy toads and big, fat bats,
Shaking bones and rattling chains,
Haunted churches, dark country lanes,
It's that spooky, scary time of year,
End of October, Hallowe'en is here!
Pumpkin lights and trick or treat,
People at doors for sweets to eat.

People's doors covered in flour and eggs,
Kids running away on fast little legs,
Dressing up as a witch, or a ghost,
Trying to frighten people the most,
Then at last tucked up in bed,
Dreams of 'nasties' in their head,
Under the covers pulled up to their ears,
The children recover from their fears,
Another Hallowe'en gone, another year gone by,
Dream of Bonfire Night, watching the rockets fly.

Kim Kay (13)
King Edmund School

MADE UP

My brother
one day said
to me,
while I was putting
on my lippy,
'Why do you hide your
face so much,
and loose the natural
colour as such?'
It kind of got me thinking.
It's not the mascara that
makes the blinking,
wear the blusher to hide
embarrassment,
lipstick to hide the words
they sent,
eyeshadow for no bad
things to see,
and foundation to
hide the real, true
me.

Hannah Mumford (14)
King Edmund School

ANIMALS

Animals can be small
Animals can be sweet
Animals can be tall
Animals can be neat

Dogs, hamsters and cats
Chasing after a ball
Mice, kittens and rats
Running down the hall
Puppies, horses and bats
I *love* them all.

Jade Mills (12)
King Edmund School

A HORROR

Loud screams echo all around
If you listen to the sound
I'm sure you'll just run away
Out into the open day
If you wish to enter my house
Ask yourself am I man or mouse?
The cold chill will get to you
It gets to me too
The werewolf howls might make you scream
I bet you're thinking she's so mean
The cold walls will send a shiver down your spine
Hands off that! It's mine
Well I hope you will come back soon
Make sure you come on a full moon
Go home and tell your mum
She'll say I don't believe you son.

Jodie Norton (11)
King Edmund School

FOOTBALL

Football, football is so fun
out of the tunnel, here they come.
Liverpool, Liverpool are the best
watch the team, beat the rest.

Thousands of people watch the game
to see all the fame.
Keeper, keeper dives for the ball
but frankly dear, don't they all?

On a cold and frosty night
Liverpool play with all their might.
Scoring goals here and there
whoops! I hit his rear.

John Fitz-Gibbon (13)
King Edmund School

DARKNESS OF THE NIGHT

Glassy eyes gazed transfixed at the blanket overhead,
Star studded, twinkling, clear as the pearly luminous waters
Shimmering, shimmering.
The wrinkled face illuminated, wise and had seen many a night,
Lay resting on its velvety, feathery berth
Tranquil, tranquil.

Hercules, a potent warrior, failed the test of love,
The Big Dipper, a roller-coaster journey of emotions
Ended, ended.
For now everything is clear, clear like mountain spring waters,
I am isolated from society with only the sky as guidance,
An example of failure I wither away, slowly, slowly.

Nicola Brown (13)
King Edmund School

THINKING

I think of all the happy things,
which happened over the years.
The parties I have had, the fun
and games and not about the tears.

I try to think of my family and
all my friends too;
and all of the things I really like to do.

But then I think of bad things
which have happened in my life,
the death of Aaron and my cousin,
and the man with a knife.

I'm scared of all the bad things,
and happy about all the good.
I think this is right and I think
I should forget all the bad
and remember all the good.

Measha Emmons (12)
King Edmund School

AN INNOCENT VICTIM

An innocent victim
Alone in the rain
An innocent victim
Who lies in shame

An innocent victim
Cold and wet
An innocent victim
Who doesn't know where to go yet

This poor creature
Is all alone
This poor creature
Needs a home

He whines and moans
At passers by
And wonders why
He isn't known

He's starving, he's hungry
He's looking for food
This poor little dog
Is in such a mood

Along comes a person
And sees this dog
And takes him home in the fog.

Nicola Hill (13)
King Edmund School

FAMILY

First we start with Mum, she's our cleaner,
Who's there to do everything, for us.
I want this, I want that,
That's what I think mums are for.

Then there's dad, he's the worker of the family.
He works all day long.
When he comes home he's always saying,
'Where's my dinner, where is it?'
That's what my dad does all day long.

Then there's my sister,
She's the pain of the family.
She's always mucking around
And being silly.

Then there's my brother,
He's always on that PlayStation.
He's always up there playing on it.
It's like he's trapped in his own room.

Then last but not least, there's me.
I'm just wonderful,
I am the brains of the family.

Well that's my family.
Now I've told you about them,
I think I deserve a clap.

Claire Bush (12)
King Edmund School

I REALLY WANT SOME SWEETS

I really want some sweets,
I really want them,
I really want the treats,
But in the shop there are scary men.
I asked my mum and she said I can,
But I spent all my money,
When I bought a fan,
My mum thought it was funny,
All the men in the shop were crude,
Then my nanny,
Although the men were rude,
Gave me some money, good old granny
Then I bought the sweets
I really got the treats!

Johnathon Clark (12)
King Edmund School

MY LOST UNDERWEAR

Pots and pans flying everywhere,
This is so scary, I've lost my hair.
Now they are attacking my teddy bear,
They are giving him the evil glare.
I grab an old wooden chair,
But hit the line with the underwear.
Oh I missed, it's just not fair,
And now I've lost all my underwear.
I am going to tell Tony Blair,
About how I lost all my hair.

Michael Smith (11)
King Edmund School

SUBJECTS

English, English is cool,
nothing boring about it,
commas, full stops, question marks and hyphens,
it's not much fun sitting in silence.

Science, science is interesting,
gases, water, Bunsen burner flames,
finding out how something works,
that's our aim.

Geography, geography is very hard,
it helps you find the place you're looking for,
maps and charts, easier by far,
years ago they followed a star.

Lauren Brind (11)
King Edmund School

MY BEST FRIENDS

My best friends stand by me
When I'm in trouble or
When I'm in need for help.
Sometimes they are mean to me,
Sometimes I hate them, not really!
We make up, we break up,
We squabble and squirm,
But the most important thing is:
We always stay friends.

Linzi Cattell (11)
King Edmund School

SHADOW CREATURE

It's midnight.
The dark covers the world, like a blanket.
A bobbing shape steps out of nowhere,
its glowing eyes shining like torch beams.
The cat's fluid movement is quiet, like the wind.
Its expressionless face looks this way and that,
searching for victims.
The night is as cold as ice.
The breeze drifts through the trees
and disturbs the cat's silvery whiskers.
It looks as though they are dancing on his face.
He sits on the rough brick wall and stares into oblivion,
like a lonely statue.
And then, like there is no emotion in his silky, smooth soul,
he pads silently back to his abode.

Gemma Bright (13)
King Edmund School

THE SENSES OUTSIDE MY DOOR

The depth and the dreams
of my desire.
The sweet smelling roses
that shimmer in the sunlight.
Will I ever live in my twilight zone?
Will I feel the fog in the back of my throat?
Will I see the gathering of glorious flowers?
Will I hear the chorus of the birds?
Will I taste the ripeness of fruit?
For I cannot die till my desire is fulfilled.

Stephen Hill (11)
King Edmund School

A RAINY NIGHT IN THE WOODS

Never will I make the trip again,
To a forest in Germany with my best mate Sven.
It seemed a long trip to the centre of this wood,
When we finally got there our spot was no good.
We could not nail or pitch our tent,
The ground was too hard and our pegs just bent.
It was from this point on when I knew it would be a disaster,
So I wanted the end to come faster and faster.
We finally managed to set up a bed,
Then felt some rain dripping on my head.
We eventually managed to survive the night,
I woke in the morning with a terrible fright.
My best mate Sven being a cheeky fella,
Stayed up all night with food and umbrella.

Daniel Patmore (13)
King Edmund School

MY CAT

There she lay
asleep all day
She licks and purrs
miaows and plays
She chases dogs
and scares them away
They run a mile when
she comes to play
Her scent, her touch
they all know well
that's why
they daren't stay.

Irvana Grebovic (13)
King Edmund School

IS THIS LOVE TRUE?

I know how I feel about you,
Your looks and thoughts,
Is this love that I feel for you true?
I know that no courts,
Can keep me away from
You, can stop me feeling this love,
You can drop a bomb,
But the magical dove,
Will still appear,
And cast its spell.
You are like a frightened deer,
You do not listen to your heart's bell.
Should I approach you,
Or keep my feelings in the blue?

Victoria Handley (14)
King Edmund School

ON THE RUN

I hear their voices in the trees,
Echoing through the branches and leaves,
Shadows roaming across the hillside,
Following me to the end.
By a rock I sit and wait,
Remembering times which stay, otherwise forgotten.
Times of peace, and not of war,
When running was not forbidden,
And terror did not roam the streets.
Now it is time to face my demon,
Be captured by my greatest fears,
Do not stop for me, unless you want to,
For I am already dead, under my love for you.

Joshua Grocott (13)
King Edmund School

THE ALIENS, MICE AND THE SACK

On this planet some time ago,
Aliens landed to say hello,
But they landed next to a rotting house,
And all they found was a mouse,
Up, up they went and flew away,
But only to come back another day.

100 years later they came back,
To put all the mice in a sack,
But when they found out humans were about,
They ran away without a doubt.

No one knows if they will be back,
Or if they will bring a big sack.

Richard Fox (13)
King Edmund School

MY BIKE

I like to ride my bike
My bike I like to ride
I jump the ramps
With all its bumps
Then I crash and stack it
I am hurt but never give up
Give up will I never
The bike is called a Ruption
And full of corruption
Once new, now old
I will never forget my BMX.

Sam Elsey (13)
King Edmund School

I'M GOING ON HOLIDAY

Today I'm going on holiday
I'm flying away
On a plane
In this terrible rain

I'm delighted to say
I'm excited to go away
Up, up, up in the sky
I've always wanted to fly

I can go in the hot
I will love it a lot
The aeroplane is big
And look, the waitress wears a wig

I'm packing my clothes
For this good old holiday
I'm flying away
Oh what a day!

Holly Clark (11)
King Edmund School

WAR

Sound of guns firing,
People dying on the ground.
Flame-throwers, people frying,
Fire blazing in your eyes,
Destruction all around.
Sounds of people getting crushed,
By heavy tanks that soon were hushed.
An atom bomb came flying down,
Everyone dead all around.

David Stapleton (11)
King Edmund School

THE FINAL BREATH

Now I sit here, head held low,
Hoping there's not far to go.
As I settle into the road of life well trod,
Sitting here just thinking and praying to God.

Knowing I have my life to defend,
Hoping I finish before the end.
Wishing there was a new way to start,
Knowing there isn't breaking my heart.

No way of knowing when to die,
Now telling the truth no more need to lie.
Knowing I can't last much longer,
Feeling the love, making me stronger.

Not knowing how much more I can take,
Holding on for everyone's sake.
Then I settle down for the night,
Knowing that I'm going to lose this fight.

Closing my eyes waiting for death,
Then I take my final breath.

Sharron Ibbitson (15)
Robert Clack School

MY POEM

This is my poem,
I don't know what about.
I'm writing down what I'm thinking,
To try to get it all out.

Whatever comes into my head,
I write it down straight away.
And when I put pen to paper,
Don't stop me. I'm away.

I'm trying to get it out,
But I don't think it's working.
If I could only tape this,
All ready I can feel it working.

It's nearly the end of my poem,
It's time to say goodbye.
I'm not really good at this,
But here it goes. *Bye! Bye!*

Luke Tyson (11)
St Clere's GM School

JELLYFISH

Jellyfish, jellyfish how you sparkle like the night.
as you slither and slime through the sand.
And how you glisten like the sunshine and the pure whiteness
of your skin.
Your long beautiful tentacles dangle by your side.
They feel like smooth golden silk.
How beautiful you are.
Jellyfish, jellyfish.

Benjamin Lisgarten (11)
St Clere's GM School

I Wish . . .

I wish I could fly up high,
With the birds in the sky,
I wish I could swim in the sea,
With all the fish surrounding me,
I'd swim with dolphins, whales and fish,
And this would be my only wish,
To see all the animals set free,
Instead of living in captivity.

If all animals could be set free,
What a wonderful place this would be,
There'd be more tigers, lions and birds,
All animals would live in great herds.
Herds of an enormous number,
When they walked it would sound like thunder,

There'd be no more zoos and places like that,
Places to cage all the wild cats,
Big cats should be left on the plains,
Especially lions with their big bushy manes,
Poaching I would totally ban,
And I would have a secret plan,
To stop their evil scheme,
It really is quite mean
They sell tiger paws,
And leopards' claws,
It really should be stopped,
Before all the animals are locked up or shot,

Remember animals were here before us,
So what we should do is give them our love,
Before I go please spread the word,
To save every creature, animals and bird.

Nicole Moon (13)
St Clere's GM School

MY DEEPEST THOUGHTS ON SEASONS

The days become more gloomy,
The clouds darken and become full,
It's coming near to the time that snow will fall.
Sitting here upon my desk,
Looking upon the rooftops,
Watching cats play and birds hunt for scraps.
The summer becomes a faint memory.
As the nights darken and autumn comes.

When the leaves fall from the trees,
As the phantom of darkness passes,
The nights get darker and scarier.
Walking through the streets seeing all of the changes,
Time passes and next on the agenda is winter.

The coldest part of the year,
I'm still walking through the streets,
But now another change has occurred.
Snowflakes are falling softly to the ground,
And leaving a pale white carpet behind.
Winter is cold,
Although it makes me feel warm inside.

Now spring springs up from nowhere,
Things brighten up and the memory of summer becomes clearer.
New creatures are born everywhere,
And the delightful smell of flowers can be smelt.
Snow gets melted away.
And as if my magic the sun shines brightly,
And pushes away the wind and rain,
Until summer falls again.

As the memories of summer,
Come flooding back,
I can make a fresh start,
And watch the deep blue waves wash away
the golden sand,
on the beach,
and my footprints disappear,
just like the seasons,
until they begin all over again.

Karen Martin (13)
St Clere's GM School

MY GRANDMA HAS THE FASTEST PURSE IN THE WEST!

When I'm not being a pest,
My grandma has the fastest purse in the west!
When I work hard and pass a test,
My grandma has the fastest purse in the west!

When I'm better than all the rest,
My grandma has the fastest purse in the west!
She sees me as amongst the best,
My grandma has the fastest purse in the west!

I'm the youngest one in her nest,
My grandma has the fastest purse in the west!
So she bought me a knitted string vest,
My grandma has the fastest purse in the west!

When I'm not a pest,
and being the best,
out of the rest,
wearing my vest,
the youngest of her nest,
My grandma definitely has the fastest purse in the west!

Emily Catchpole (12)
St Clere's GM School

MY BIRTHDAYS

Today it's my birthday,
Hip hip hooray!
Staring at that cake all day.
My oh my, is that the time?
Time to party, time for fun,
Boogying all night long,
Listen to that beating drum
Bang! Bang! Bang!
Thump! Thump! Thump!
Thudding feet, it's time to eat!
Yum! Yum! Yum!
Scrum! Scrum! Scrum!
I love cake in my tum.

Laura Martin (11)
St Clere's GM School

THE UNICORN

In the night about twelve o'clock
You'll hear the unicorn run non-stop.
But if you are lucky enough to see
You'll see the pure white coat as smooth as can be.
With his long white tail that flows like silk.
And his lovely mane the colour of milk,
But the twisted horn above his head is so beautiful it can't be said,
And as he runs he doesn't make a sound,
Just the rustling of the leaves that lay scattered on the ground.

Lauren Shea (12)
St Clere's GM School

WHAT THE WORLD LOOKED LIKE

Yellow flowers like daffodils,
Which everyone adores.
They come out in the summertime,
And mean so much to me.
You handle them very carefully,
Because of their fragility.
I love the colour,
The golden colour,
With greeny colour leaves.

Then there's the lilies,
Floating on the pond.
They must be so happy,
Resting all day long!
Frogs leaping in and out,
That's the way I like it.

Other people pick the flowers,
Which smell lovely to this day.
Flowers make the world look nice.
But just remember to think twice,
Before the world becomes destroyed,
And people forget,
What the world looked like.

Charlotte Furze (12)
St Clere's GM School

TAKE-OVER

Someone's looking through my eyes,
My mouth is talking, telling lies.
Part of me says 'Just be happy,'
Part of me says 'Just be sad.'
I'm confused, bewildered even stunned,
'Till I think I'm going mad.

Who's controlling my heart, liver, lungs and brain?
Who can touch, hear and see?
Makes me think I'm going insane,
Like something's got control of me.

Have you ever tried not thinking?
It's a hard thing to do.
You try to do one thing,
And your brain will do the other.
It's just like having,
An annoying sister or brother.

Neil Smith (12)
St Clere's GM School

WHY?

Why is it that people have to suffer before death?
Why is it that everything good has to end?
Why is it that people get scared of the world we all live in?
Why is it that cruelty takes place within us?
Why is it that love can be so cruel?
Why is it that sharing causes arguments?
Why is it that peace feels so far away from existence?
Does it feel like we, us, can make our world a warmer place to be?

Laura Archer (12)
St Clere's GM School

THE ULTIMATE DILEMMA

I have sailed the calm ocean,
Docked at the harbour.
Walked through the busy streets,
Out of the city where signposts show the way.
I now stand in a dimly lit forest.
Before me a fork in the road to negotiate.
To the right, a busy, yet eerily calm road.
A road upon which many of my friends walk.
To the left a muddy path,
A continuation of the path upon which I stand,
A path with many twists and turns,
And the occasional obstacle to overcome.
The few walk this turbulent road,
Yet in the distance I see my mother, my siblings, my aunt.
I shall take this path,
I shall tackle every challenge,
For I do enjoy the finish,
Knowing that I have tried my hardest throughout,
And have come out victorious.
Hopefully successful in *life*.

Thomas Griffin (15)
St Thomas More School

NAMES

My mother's name is Sally,
My father's name is Jim.
My sister's name is Megan,
Who's 5ft 6" and slim.

My auntie's name is Helen,
My uncle's name is Paul.
My cousin's name is Linda,
And that's not nearly all.

For my grandma's name is Enid,
My grandpa's name is Ned.
There was great uncle Albert,
But now, I'm afraid he's dead!

My best friend's name is Tina,
Whose best friend's name is Jean.
My other friend is Andy,
And his brother's name is Dean.

My teacher's name is Lorna,
Who married Mr Right.
Their daughter's name is Gina,
Who of course is rather bright!

And now down to the secrets,
Of all the names above.
I'll be honest and be truthful,
Of who they really love!

Now Megan fancies Andy,
Who's rather keen on Jean.
She actually loves Johnny,
Who's the cousin of Andy and Dean!

And Tina, she hates Johnny,
It's a true and total fact.
But Johnny he *likes* Tina,
Oh dear, he'll need some tact!

Now you know the secrets,
Of my funny family tree.
I'd really better go now,
It's nearly time for tea.

Evelyn Waite (12)
The Sanders Draper School

NONSENSE POEM

One 'boaring' day I had nothing to do,
I decided to visit Colchester Zoo.
I saw a giraffe with a very sore throat,
And corns on the feet of a mountain goat.
In the reptile house there was a 'hissterical' snake,
And a crocodile crying with bad toothache.
The ostrich was trying with all his might,
But as much as he tried he could not take flight.
There was a skunk sitting all alone,
And his nasty smell 'scent' me home.

Adam Kennedy (12)
The Sanders Draper School

MY FAMILY

I'm going to write you a poem,
Of my family and what they do.
I'm going to write you a poem,
So here it goes, my family for you.

My mum works in a school kitchen,
She washes each tray by tray.
Cleans up the hall after food fights,
And the kids run out and play.

My dad is an electrician,
He connects circuits wire by wire.
If he doesn't wear his rubber boots,
He electrocutes and catches on fire.

Sister number one goes to college,
Sister number two goes to school.
They are both really annoying,
And are not important at all.

Grandad one is lots of fun,
And is a crazy golfer.
Grandad two is a smoking loon,
And golfs all day like a loner.

Both my nannies are really good cooks,
I don't know whose food is finer.
Nanny P's afters and nanny B's roast,
Is better than a meal at the diner.

Then I have great nanny Jackson,
Jackson her last name of course.
She lives all the way up in Lincoln
And her hair and her teeth are false.

That is all my close family,
All except for me.
I am the greatest one of all,
As it is clear to see.

Courtney Purse (12)
The Sanders Draper School

MY PUPPY

I have a little puppy
Alfie, that's his name.
He chews, barks, burps and parps
But I love him all the same.

He ate my sister's hairdryer
My dad's best slippers too.
But what really gets him well told off
Is using the carpet as a loo!

'No Alfie don't be naughty,'
But he looks at me and smiles.
Then casually walks to the kitchen
And tinkles all over the tiles.

He's full of fun and mischief
He cheers up my day no end.
If you're feeling down, get a puppy
After all they are man's best friend!

Sam Oates 11)
The Sanders Draper School

MY LIFE

Every day is a challenge for me
I always try and be the best that I can possibly be.
Karate shows my power and strength
Dancing is all in my rhythm and mind
And swimming is the most relaxing activity that I can find.
The confidence I have in myself
Is built upon what I do
And it always helps to have a loving family
Who support and encourage you,
I can't imagine not doing what I do
It's just so wonderful when you can do what you love doing.
I hope people like me who have dreams, can fulfil them too.
It's just a matter of concentrating and believing in what you do.

Samantha Clark (12)
The Sanders Draper School

MY HOLIDAY

I like to go on holiday especially to Spain.
The bit I like most of all is when I'm on the plane.
I have a drink and eat a meal, and
Look up to the sky.
The clouds look like cotton wool
Because we are very high.
Then bump, we are on land again
And we begin to cheer.
We say goodbye we'll be back soon
About this time next year.

Danielle Common (12)
The Sanders Draper School

TEACHERS

They sit in the staff room drinking and eating,
Sometimes when we're lucky they have long meetings,
They tell us off, who knows why?
It's great at the end of school when we say 'Bye bye!'
It's thrilling when the holidays come,
Not so special for my poor old mum.
Teachers have favourites who are at their beck and call,
While other kids are bunking and shopping down the mall,
Teachers give homework, loads and loads and loads,
Bof jobs have cheating devices with very special codes,
Detentions are the worst you can get,
While others are out having water fights with water jets.

Lauren Tomlinson (12)
The Sanders Draper School

THE LION SONG

Why are lions always so lazy?
I look at them and think 'Oh my and they are crazy!'
Why do lions keep on yawning?
At night-time, not in the morning!

Why do lions always lie under trees?
Catching the air, sun and the breeze,
Why do lions always roar,
Whilst all the time they just sit and ignore.

Amy Jarman (12)
The Sanders Draper School

BOYS

Climbing fences,
Climbing trees,
Getting great big
Holey knees.

Cutting fingers,
Cutting thumbs.
Getting told off
By their mums.

Doing homework,
Plenty of moans.
Playing silly games,
Breaking many bones.

Dirty and clean,
The clothes they wear,
Even if they have
A great tear.

Playing football,
Rugby too,
When no homework,
They have to do.

Singing a song,
Doing a mime,
Acting silly,
And wasting
        all their time.

Amanda Harper (14)
The Sanders Draper School

I KNOW A BOY WHO'S CRAZY

I know a boy who's crazy,
I know a boy who's mad.
Some people think he's funny,
While others think he's sad.

He acts like a gorilla,
Sitting in a tree.
He says his name is Cilla,
When his name is Lee.

He always turns up late for school,
Every single day.
And when the teacher asks him why,
He says he's lost his way.

He's always talking to thin air,
Like he's talking to a friend.
And when we ask him who is there,
He says his name is Ben.

When we eat our dinner,
He eats it like a pig.
He eats it all so wildly,
It ends up as a wig.

He plays tennis with a football,
And rugby with a racket.
I think we should call the men in white,
To put him in a straightjacket.

Joe Broom (12)
The Sanders Draper School

I WENT TO A DANCE

I went to a dance,
and I fell into a trance.
I had a funny dream
that I was in a football team.
I scored a goal for England
the crowd they roared and roared.
I don't know how I managed it,
before I've never scored.
The Queen called me to the palace
and gave me lots of praise.
She noticed that upon my knee
I had a nasty graze.
She dressed it up in a bandage
and sent me on my way.
I thanked her very nicely
and asked if I could stay.
No! No! She said you silly girl
you're only in a dream.
I woke up very suddenly
with my head in the peaches and cream!
The crowd they stood around me
they said 'Are you OK?'
I said yes thank you very much
I'd best be on my way.

Gemma Luckman (12)
The Sanders Draper School

KALEIDOSCOPE

You twist the end round and round
The colours come together to make different patterns.
You try your best to work out what it is.
Can you see it?
A jumble of colours shuffling together.
The shapes of hexagons, squares and diamonds.
Can you see it?
A mystery picture sent to play with your mind.
You get frustrated but you can't put it down
Can you see it?
What could it be?
I know what it is, a
Kaleidoscope.

Rebecca Shuttleworth (12)
Shoeburyness County High School

THE KALEIDOSCOPE

My new colourful kaleidoscope that glitters in the sun.
As I put my eye to the kaleidoscope I can feel the excitement.
As I look through, the shapes are all different
When I turn it around the shapes twist and turn.
The shapes and colours swirl and swish as though they are avoiding
each other.
The colours changing every second, as the images go around
and around.
I'm losing my mind in colours!

Laura Brooks (12)
Shoeburyness County High School

KALEIDOSCOPE

My kaleidoscope is so much fun,
Many patterns, many colours,
Yellow, blue, brown and red,
It's all buzzing round my head,
All shapes, all sizes
Rectangles, circles, squares, hexagons,
And many more.
My kaleidoscope is so much fun,
Many patterns, many colours,
Colourful and bright,
Dazzling and light.
Flashing through the night,
I like my kaleidoscope.

Joanne Pattison (12)
Shoeburyness County High School

THE BOY

When I walk into school,
He's standing there,
With his bright green jacket,
All unaware.
I reach out to touch his face,
And his freckles trying to escape.
His hair all dark and curly
Shapes and patterns reoccurring.
He has a nose shaped like a cherry
And when he smiles he makes me merry.
He makes me feel on top of the world
And makes my heart all fulfilled.

Kelly Wall (13)
Shoeburyness County High School

THE PRESENT

The time has come,
Frantic, rushing must be first,
Find it quick I know it's here,
It's here, my name.
A cylinder attached,
Confused what can it be?
A blue cylinder lays before me,
A window to a new world - I peered in,
I was startled at what I saw,
I twisted it, the colours changed before my eyes,
Reds and blues, pinks and greens danced before me,
I kept twisting, the pattern kept changing,
I looked, it changed, I looked again,
The constantly changing world of colours,
The patterns changed and reformed.
I sat there entranced,
A vast universe of patterns opened up before me,
Like stained glass falling into place,
The intricate images dazzled and amazed me,
As they appeared and vanished
I watched with awe,
What a wonderful gift,
The kaleidoscope.

Danyka Barke (12)
Shoeburyness County High School

A SHAPE IN THE DISTANCE

In the distance,
Saw a light,
I went near,
Couldn't believe my eyes!

There lay a clear glass shape,
A very weird shape,
Maybe it was a hexagon,
Maybe it was even an octagon,
I didn't bother looking at this shape,
But concentrated on the thing that was in it.

It was a little girl,
Sleeping cosy and tight,
With her eyes closed.

She had long blonde hair,
Which swept across her face,
She had the beauties of a star,
Far more beautiful than you and I,
She seemed like a princess,
Who had run away,
And somehow ended up in a glass shaped case.

She had the face of an angel,
An angel who had flown onto the ground,
With her wings hanging behind.

Maybe I was imagining things,
But there was a part of me,
Which said;
I had seen what there was to be seen.

Rukhshana Khalique (13)
Shoeburyness County High School

EARTH

People die every day,
Animals, plants, anyway,
But one big place that is dying,
Is the earth and I'm not lying.
Fire, volcanoes, earthquakes the lot,
Soon the world will be boiling hot,
With all the gas,
And oil in the sea,
Soon it will be the end of you and me.
People don't care about the Earth,
And soon we won't be able to surf,
Or do the things we used to do,
So help the earth, me and you,
Instead of going in the car,
Walk a little, it won't be far.
Recycle paper, plastic, glass,
Look at the future,
Not at the past.

Chloe Haddow (13)
Shoeburyness County High School

KALEIDOSCOPE

A kaleidoscope is long and thin
You twist and turn
It's made of tin.
Pretty patterns turning around
Red, yellows, greens and browns.
Twist again and it will change,
If you like them you will see
Pretty patterns will appear,
They may even seem clear.

Natalie Keyes (12)
Shoeburyness County High School

KALEIDOSCOPE

I look through a hole,
I see,
Pinks, reds, yellows, greens, blues,
Squares, ovals, triangles, diamonds,
Dancing before my eye.
I twist and turn it, now I see more and,
More different colours of different,
Shapes and sizes.

Blues and whites.
Blue, blue as the ocean,
White, white as ripples in the water,
Reds and pinks.
Red, red as blood pure as redcurrant,
Pink, pink pure as punch,
And juicy as a grapefruit,
Greens and yellows.
Green, green as grass, rich as a holly bush,
Yellow, yellow as the sun;
Smooth as butter and sticky as,
Caramel.

Harriet Penasa (12)
Shoeburyness County High School

KALEIDOSCOPE

Round and round my tube they go
Colours rocking to and fro.
Twist me to the left and right
A maze of colours, all in flight
Hold me up to the light to see
Now can you guess what I can be?

Adam Bawden (13)
Shoeburyness County High School

CAMPING WITH MY KALEIDOSCOPE

Going through the bumpy hillside,
Kaleidoscope by my side.
Set up camp, getting dark now,
Clouds floating overhead,
Dark, pitch-black, getting cold.
But wait! What's this light?
Could it be . . . ?
It's changing colour,
What is it?
Twisting and turning, making
Patterns in the sky,
That catch my eye like millions,
Of jewel stones floating by.
Of course my kaleidoscope, that's what it is!
Whoever invented it, is a real whiz!

Louisa Bailey (12)
Shoeburyness County High School

KALEIDOSCOPE

You have to look into me,
Twist me round,
But the bad thing about me is,
there isn't any sound.
I'm red and green and white and blue,
and whatever colour you really choose.
You can pick me up,
Put me down,
You can even wear me as your crown,
You can't use me as your soap,
I'm a *kaleidoscope.*

Phillip Cruickshank (12)
Shoeburyness County High School

KALEIDOSCOPE

As I tip-toed closer
Into my room,
Thinking of everything
Including the tune.

I know what I want
My exciting toy,
Eventually I lift it
And slowly, I look right in.

Nothing, nothing,
What do I see,
I'm really disappointed,
I'm looking at white.

What's this I see?
A multicoloured wheel,
So I turned it
And looked in again.

The shapes, squares and circles,
The colours, blue and red,
And I was hooked,
From breakfast to bed.

Daniel Rivers (14)
Shoeburyness County High School

THE STRANGE OBJECT

As you stare in the scope
It twists and twirls
It is fascinating
The alien object flashes and flares
It has colours bursting out at you
Pink
Purple
Red
Orange
Blue
Green
It is a magical object
With twisting and twirling shapes inside
It is everything a child wants
In a tatty old tube.

Paul Bean (12)
Shoeburyness County High School

KALEIDOSCOPE

Pink, red, yellow and blue,
See how many colours you can see when you look through.
Maybe circles, maybe squares, patterns, patterns everywhere.

Don't take too long, I want a go,
I want to see that shining glow,
I want it to be bright,
Although I expect it might,
Kaleidoscope, kaleidoscope, please come within my sight.

Samantha McDonald (12)
Shoeburyness County High School

KALEIDOSCOPE

A kaleidoscope shape is cylindrical,
with patterns inside symmetrical.

Colours of the rainbow small and bright,
shapes to the left and shapes to the right.

The patterns remind me of the firework show,
hold it up to the light and watch it glow.

A constantly changing set of colours,
revolving patterns made by pieces of glass.

Turn it, turn it, turn it around,
an ever-changing merry-go-round.

Adam Miller (12)
Shoeburyness County High School

KALEIDOSCOPE

I look through a kaleidoscope, guess what I see,
I see colours, patterns,
That's what I see.

Patterns, different patterns,
Colours, different colours,
Colours like red, blue and pink,
Patterns like diamonds, circles, hexagons,
and many more.
Kaleidoscope, kaleidoscope I want to see,
If you don't believe, you go and see.

Linzi Carrington (12)
Shoeburyness County High School

INSIDE THE BOX

A young girl, of about five, brushes her long, blonde, silky hair
as she rushes up the stairs of the old house towards the playroom.
She gets an old, dusty wooden box and opens it,
only her very best things go in the ancient box.
The girl takes out a silver, tin cylinder object,
a kaleidoscope, her favourite toy.
She has got the chance to play on computers or sit in front of a
television all day,
but she prefers to play with this incredible toy.
The girl picks up the kaleidoscope and walks over to a tall window
with colourful curtains hanging on it.
She puts her dark blue eye to the eye-piece of the kaleidoscope and
held it up to where the sun was shining.
It was a perfect day to play with this brilliant thing,
inside, she could see all of the colours of the rainbow:
Red, blue, yellow, orange, green and purple with the plain black
background, probably to make the colourful shapes stand out.
The shapes looked like four snowflakes, but when it is turned, they
formed something that looked like one big snowflake.
'How does it work?' the girls asks herself, 'Is it magic?'
That is something she will never know, but she knows that she will
never
get bored of this marvellous, astounding object.
She will have to force herself away from this remarkable kaleidoscope.

Emma Sheehan (12)
Shoeburyness County High School

KALEIDOSCOPE

I am sitting on the grass
And I look at the sky
I see the colours changing.

I am still looking at the sky
I saw the patterns changing.
As I looked closer
It looked like a kaleidoscope.

As I kept on trying
To see the colours and patterns
I realised
It was only the sky.

Katie Hanger (13)
Shoeburyness County High School

KALEIDOSCOPE

I have a little kaleidoscope,
It makes different patterns.
I turn it around to see what happens.

It looks like a kite,
The colours are nice and bright
What a wonderful sight
I get when I hold it up to the light.

Lucy-Marie Lovell (12)
Shoeburyness County High School

KALEIDOSCOPE

I look into a kaleidoscope,
I see the magic,
I see beautiful shapes colliding,
I see brilliantly bright shapes and colours,
I see weird symmetry,
I see the magic in the kaleidoscope.

When I twist the changing knob,
I see another magic pattern,
Every pattern is unique in its own way.

Jeff Lane (13)
Shoeburyness County High School

KALEIDOSCOPE

When I look into my kaleidoscope I can't really see much else
But lots of little coloured bits waving around
making patterns on the ground.
Colours and colours flashing around
making patterns like stained glass.
Colours fly in and out of your eyes,
You can see feint objects flash with colour.
I love kaleidoscopes, don't you?

Charlotte O'Brien (12)
Shoeburyness County High School

KALEIDOSCOPE

A kaleidoscope is special
It has more colours than a rainbow,
Makes more patterns than a chameleon.
A kaleidoscope is special
You put your eye to the rim
Then the fun will begin.
A kaleidoscope is special
Let your imagination run wild
Like an excited little child.
A kaleidoscope is special.

James O'Dell (13)
Shoeburyness County High School

KALEIDOSCOPE

Red, yellow, orange and blue
All mixed together in a pattern or two.

Hot colours, cold colours,
Bright colours, bold colours.
So if you can't cope
Look at this wonderful

      Kaleidoscope!

Sarah Davis (12)
Shoeburyness County High School

KALEIDOSCOPE

My brother's birthday is on Tuesday,
He wants something exciting.
I went to the toy shop,
I looked here, looked there,
But nothing could I find,
Until I saw something flash,
I saw it glisten, I saw it twinkle.
'Excuse me sir but how much is that?'
He looked and smiled,
'Aye er that's a good buy at 46 pence,'
'Thank you sir,'
I took it to the counter,
'That will be 46 pence please,'
I handed over a new and shiny 50 pence piece,
He put it in a bag and gave me the change,
I walked home and wrapped the present,
And hid it under my mattress.
Oh Tuesday please come quick,
For you see I am no good at keeping secrets.

Friday, Saturday, Sunday,
Then Monday came,
Mother baked the cake and sent us to bed.
My brother awoke very early next morn,
'Happy birthday' I said as I passed it to him,
He fumbled with the string and tore at the paper,
'I love it,' he said.

Elizabeth Bull (13)
Shoeburyness County High School

KALEIDOSCOPE

I'm going mad!
If I don't get out of here
I'm going to have a mental breakdown.
It's confusing me seeing a different pattern after pattern.
What's going on?
I feel like I'm trying to break out of my head.
Help me please! I'm in here,
Help me break free.
It's no use, they can't hear.
Wait, what's happening?
I'm twisting around, I'm seeing red,
No green, no blue.
I feel really dizzy,
I can't stand it.
Help me escape,
Please!

Charlotte Smyth (12)
Shoeburyness County High School

AN AMAZING KALEIDOSCOPE

All different colours that change when you twist,
They're like twinkling lights you can see in a mist.
The shapes make a picture like people in a city,
Some shapes are smooth but others are gritty.
The amazing colours whizzing around and around,
Some stand upwards and others face down.
So many different colours I find it hard to count,
How much there actually is in the final amount.

Rosa Donoghue (13)
Shoeburyness County High School

FIRST DAY AT SENIOR SCHOOL

'Don't worry,
You'll be fine.'
I enter (the prison)
Slowly I walk through the corridor,
Will I survive?
A shudder runs down my spine,
The thud of my footsteps echo through the corridor.
The lino lurks at my feet,
The pale pink walls close in,
I shudder violently.
The grey day drags on,
The day soon turns blue,
It comes to an end,
I exit the prison . . . er . . . school
I feel free
It's over!

Josie Collins (13)
The Chafford School

I AM AS NORMAL AS YOU

I am as normal as you.
But the difference is that I have two homes.
My dad's home
My mum's home
Sometimes it is hard for me,
Because I have to obey two sets of rules.
My dad's rules are different,
From my mum's rules.

Fiona Kenny (12)
The Chafford School

THE BEACH

I paced up and down the beach searching
Where are they?
I heard the waves hitting the shore
All around me people were happy
Not me
I could hear cheerful voices
But couldn't understand them
Where are they?
I searched across the big beach
Too big
No sign of them
The taste of salt lingered in my mouth
I shivered
I hadn't a towel
The sun glowed down on me
But still I was cold
Hours passed, seemed like years
Still no sign of them
Then in the distance
I saw a woman with curly blonde hair
A man with short brown hair
My mum and my dad!
I'd found them!

Leila Garner (12)
The Chafford School

FRIENDSHIP IS . . .

Friendship is . . .
Friendship is helping each other
Friendship is sticking up for each other
Friendship is going out with each other
Friendship is having fun
Friendship is not telling if they did something bad

Friendship is . . .
Friendship is giving each other advice
Friendship is telling each other secrets
Friendship is not taking their things
Friendship is not breaking up over silly little things

Friendship is . . .
Friendship is talking to them
Friendship is buying them presents
Friendship is sleeping round each other's houses when bad things
happen at home
Friendship is spending most of your life with them.

Lorna Crispin (13)
The Chafford School

ANGER IS . . .

Anger is when people call me names
Anger is when people take my stuff
Anger is when people pick on me
Anger is when Dad doesn't give me anything
Anger is when I don't get any money
Anger is when people copy me
Anger is when I lose a football match
Anger is when I see Arsenal lose
Anger is when I keep losing on a fighting game
Anger is when I am grounded
Anger is when I can't see Arsenal play
Anger is when I get accused of things I haven't done.
Anger is . . .

Nicky Sutton (12)
The Chafford School

BLACK POEM

Black is the colour that's mysterious at night,
black is the colour that gives you a fright.

Black is the pupils in your eyes,
black is the sound of terrifying cries.

Black is the cat that walks the wall,
black is the colour that terrifies all.

Black is the dull the dark the sadness,
black is the colour that leads to madness.

Black is the evil that waits behind the door,
black is the death that will live forever more.

Kathryn Butcher (13)
The Greensward School

FOLLOWED

Dreams are easily followed,
Ambition easily swallowed,
More often than not consumed,
But the dream always resumed.
Follow.

You know he's there
He won't try to hide
Prickly on your neck hair.
You run, at least you tried.
Followed.

It's funny to watch it fail,
The cat chasing its tail.
A serious message within
To wipe the temporary grin.
Follow.

To follow a trend
To itself does lend,
A dangerous passion,
For a thing called fashion.
Followed.

The question that lies here in verse,
Is who follows who.
The hunter becomes the hunted,
This caution I lay upon you.
Followed.

Gavin Horner (17)
The Greensward School

WHEN I WAS YOUNG

When I was young I used to want to be a pilot,
To sit at the front of a plane
And to fly hundreds of people around.
Or even better, to fly a fighter plane and to shoot the enemy craft down,
That would be brilliant.
I mean could you imagine,
Speeding through the air at 600 miles per hour,
Trying to shake off the enemy.
To fly with the birds and be in the blue sky between the
different formations of clouds.
It would be quite a responsibility, but an amazing experience.
I remember when I went on holiday once, and I went in an aeroplane.
Ah, it was so relaxing. The feeling of having no support, you were
just hanging in mid-air.
But the best part of flying for me would have to have been the
taking off and the landing of the craft.
When you took off, you'd be going really slowly whilst you taxied
on to the runway. Then you stop.
Wooossshhh! You'd go really fast and the G-Force would push you
into the back of your chair, and it would be a real effort to try and
pull yourself forward.
Landing would be even better. One minute, everything would be fine
and then, all of a sudden you would go down but your stomach would
be on the ceiling somewhere, it was really weird. Then you could see
the runway coming closer to you and you think you're going to crash
when you would suddenly get picked up, when the ship touched
the floor.

When you got used to that you would think that you've landed, then there would be a bump and you would be really shocked because you already thought that you had landed.

But that was a long time ago. Now I want to be fire-fighter, I mean could you imagine going into a room with blazing flames, firing up at you . . . but I suppose that would be a different story.

Keiran Donovan (13)
The Greensward School

MUSIC

Music to dance to,
Music to play,
Music at night,
Music at day.
Tapes, CDs, radios too,
Stamp to the beat,
Anything will do.
Clap your hands,
Jump in the air,
Dance on your own,
Or dance in a pair.
Wiggle those hips,
And swing to the groove.
Wave your arms,
Just dance and move,
Play it loud and sing along,
Jazz and pop,
What's your favourite song?

Claire Cross (14)
The Greensward School

ALIENS

Come quick, come quick,
There's one in my bed,
One what, one what?
My mother said,
Look, look,
It's walking around,
It's making such a peculiar sound,
Dip, dip, dip, dop,
It's talking to me,
Mother, Mother come and see,
Jwazzle, jwazzle,
Oh dear, oh dear,
It's made a yellow beam appear,
I need to see what the yellow beam is,
I know I'll touch it, *ooh . . . whiz*,
It's beamed me up I don't know where I am,
Suddenly I've got a craving for chocolate and ham,
But then I wake up,
It's just a dream,
Oh what's that?
It's a yellow beam!

Emma Barnard (13)
The Greensward School

SCHOOL

School, school who needs school,
With maths, English and science too,
Starts at ten to nine,
Finishes at half past three,
What a boring six hours time,
That passes like a slowing tortoise,
With only two breaks for rest,
Then it's back to the teacher's best

Lessons last one hour long,
While teachers sing their education song,
To the thirty pupils who sit in their seats,
Wishing that time could fly,
Waiting for half past three.

Craig Evans (14)
The Greensward School

THE WOLF

The silent hunter of the night
can kill its prey with a single bite
with deep brown eyes and sensitive ears
and shiny white teeth as sharp as shears.

She runs through the forest on stealthy feet
looking for something tasty to eat
and then when the opportunity comes
she hunts and chases her prey, which runs
trying desperately to get away
to live and fight another day.

But she's too fast for her potential dinners
because she is one of nature's finest killers.

But this is the point you should remember
it is the wolf, not you who is in danger.

So do not destroy these mysterious creatures
with stunning grace and beautiful features.
This is the wolf, do not take fright
she is the spirit of the night.

Russell Webster (14)
The Greensward School

UNTITLED

Closed, tight shut
An enveloping darkness stirs,
Like a feline
It masterfully preys,
As the tender blindness seizes the soul.

Views are no more,
Here landscapes remain as a memory
That cajole and coax
A gnawing thirst, that
Without remorse goes on

Sensations in shadows
Electrifying the mind.
Droplets, falling,
Settling,
Cooling.
More treasured when concealed.

A piercing twitter
Plays like a child,
Whirring and weaving,
Tempting and teasing
Emerges, advances, enlightening.

No colours. No light.
No dusk. No dawn.
Flashes of gold, spring from the heart,
A comforting chill,
Safety of secrecy locks away home.

Deprived of tradition
Innocence grows.
Fresh experiences of what has been,
Enlighten, confuse and amaze.

Seeing deprives all of emotion,
Ravishing pictures destroyed by the orbs
That unlock the world, filters it through.
Stinging sensations warm the nerves,
Not frightening, enticing, odd.

Stop. Listen, feel but don't look.
Never accept what is first perceived.
The splashes of water change in the murk,
To fantastical spells
Casting their calibre,
Tenfold.

Jennifer Drummond (17)
The Greensward School

POEMS ARE SO HARD

Poems are so hard,
So very hard to do,
They make my brain scramble,
Then turn to mushy goo.

Poems are so hard,
They are impossible,
They turn me all frustrated,
I see red like a bull.

Poems are so hard,
They are so difficult,
That when I have to do one . . .

I scream!

Ashley Brooker (14)
The Greensward School

HIGH FLIGHT

The day I was chosen to fly, boy I nearly died
To touch such a beautiful sky, I almost cried
Afterburners roaring, radios blasting
Screaming across the skies, breaking the sound barrier
What a wonderful sensation to be in this Harrier.

Chasing the frightened wind
And throwing my eager craft across the footless halls of air
Spinning dizzily
Loop to loop
Turning and turning
Suddenly easing out
To finish my exercise
To ask for permission
To take this
'Low on fuel'
Craft
Back home
To go to bed
Ready to be fed.

Kevin Hill (14)
The Greensward School

DEPRESSION

life's too difficult
can't forget
it always will be
no real reason
but every reason

people judge
people hurt
society shuns
the world's too harsh

trust nothing
care for nothing
love nothing
fear everything

why bother?
can't be bothered
stay in bed
shut out life.

Amy Fitzgerald (17)
The Greensward School

POEM ABOUT LEIGH-ON-SEA

Leigh-on-Sea is one of my favourite places to be.
There are so many things for you to do and see.
To be at the beach watching children go swimming or playing in
the mud.
Walking round the Broadwalk looking at the shops, or watching the
cockle men unloading their boats.
But once a year old Leigh really comes alive. It's the regatta, there's
music, games, food and many events to watch.
There's the greasy pole you watch someone try to climb up.
But they always fall to their humiliation.
My favourite thing to do is to go sailing.
The thrill of racing is to win at someone else's loss, which rarely
happens.
Or just to wander with your friends.
Not worrying where you are going or how you get there.
And that's why Leigh is my favourite and the only place to be.

Tom Brill (14)
The Greensward School

BEGINNING OF THE END

As my soul freezes inside my body,
My spirit is set free.
I remember no pain,
But my heart is aching.
I am caught between forgotten and remembered,
I want to scream, but there is no sound.

Where is the man, the cross, the garden?
Where is the cloud, the friend, the dream?
I am not lost, but neither am I found.
There are no problems, which in its own way is worrying,
But I am calm, not at peace.

I have arrived in no fantasy,
There are no lyrics of song,
I cannot see, hear or taste, but I feel safe.
It is not light, nor is it dark,
I am not lifted, nor am I blessed,
But I am happy, I think, with the memories I have left.

I wish I was flying and I had wings,
Like the way I thought of it in my dreams.
Where is the sun, where is the rain?
Was it just hoping, or did I believe in vain?
I do not love, I do not hate,
I have confidence in promise, but am now suspicious of my fate.

I am nervous, but not in fear,
I thought I was immortal, I was wrong.
It didn't hurt though, only the people left behind are crying,
In the beginning of the end.

Hannah Frost (17)
The Greensward School

Superhuman Force

An inaudible whisper, drifts from afar,
Spreading dread and anguish on all it touches,
The wind whips up and women cry,
This deadly force threatens tranquillity.
Warning sounds echo throughout the town,
He's everyone's nightmare, repeated again.

The shattering violence clashes down
And the people run to take cover
There is nowhere to go and nowhere to hide
He can hunt you out, feeling no guilt.
This whisper's turning venomous,
Deadly and frenzied, but cunning in his path.

Everywhere trepidation,
Accompanying agitation
Rooftops clashing,
Houses smashing,
Children wailing,
Courage failing.

He quickly moves on to seize another
People salvage whatever they can
It's nearly over and hope is found,
The inaudible whisper soon disappears.
It could not be foreseen,
So how could you escape?

He left utter chaos in his wake
Heads full of remorse and hearts like lead,
The fear of another,
And grief for the dead.
The town is reasonably peaceful now,
Life begins again, it's a question of how.

Hannah Raven (17)
The Greensward School

THE WHITE STAR LINE

People gather around the dock,
To see a marvellous spectacle.
Voices buzzing and whimpers of fear,
Fill the sea air.
As the 'Upper Class' walked onto the miracle,
All you could hear were screams of cheers.
No matter how large the floating liner was,
There was still a claustrophobic tension in the air.

Halfway through the journey a rumour spread the ship,
Whether to believe it or not was another thing.
Once the announcement was made it was all clear,
Screams of fear spread across the sea.
The cold harsh wind drowned the shouting and panic,
So the passengers felt alone in a dark underworld.

As the large liner began to sink,
The terrors on children's faces were distressing.
How could such a powerful ship with great class,
Soon be plummeting to the bottom of the sea's darkest ocean?

Passengers dived off the edge of the wrecked miracle,
Screaming as they soared into the frost-bitten salty sea.
Terrified casualties in the water watched the indestructible liner snap
in half,
While others lay dead with only a lifebelt around them to keep
them afloat.

Now we look back on the disaster as another date on the calendar,
But for the survivors it is much more.
Sitting somewhere on the sea bed,
Is the most famous liner in the world,
The Titanic.

Laura White (14)
The Greensward School

A WORLD FOR THE FUTURE

What will it be like,
Ten years from now?
I wish we could find out,
I just don't know how!

Will it be green
Healthy and alive?
Will it be clean
So we can survive?

I picture a world,
A world full of woe,
The truth unfurled,
Do you want to know?

Will it be light,
Stars in the sky?
Will it be right?
I just don't know why.

A whole melting pot,
A united planet,
When will it stop?
Living life under granite.

A bleak, dark day,
Will follow for sure.
Work out a way
To open that door.

A door to a new world,
Healthy and clean,
No chance of this,
You'll see what I mean!

Kylie Thompson (14)
The Greensward School

ARSENAL

Highbury the theatre of dreams,
The showcase for many great teams,
None so great as the Gunners themselves,
Into their history I now shall delve.

I'll start at the beginning, 1929,
In the FA Cup we did more than fine.
In fact they won, Cliff Bastin and Co,
What would happen from there no one would know.

Now to the year 1993,
Where Tony Adams rules supreme,
He helped to prove Arsenal were best,
They won the double ahead of the rest.

1994, brought European glory,
Alan Smith the head of the story.
He scored the only goal in the 21st minute,
His sweet volley ensured we would win it.

You can't talk about Arsenal without Wright,
A great goal scorer who brought such delight.
One hundred and eighty-two goals to top Bastin,
He may now have left, but Arsenal fans love him.

1998, our first Premier success,
Arsenal prove they are the best.
Beating Man U home and away,
Proving Arsenal are here to stay.

Gary Walkling (14)
The Greensward School

IF I WAS . . .

If I was a teacher I'd call my school the Fluff Academy,
We'd work ten to two,
No parents' evenings, not ever,
We'd have Ainsley in kitchen,
Dale Winton washing up,
We'd have Leonardo teaching PE,
And Denise Van Outen as well,
Paul Nicholls teaching drama.
Oh wouldn't it be fun?
We'd be a star-gazed school,
The coolest school around,
The uniform quite decent,
The best around the town.
No ties, no blazers or V-necked jumpers,
Only T-shirts, shorts, and mini skirts.

If I was an actress I'd only work with megastars,
Five million pounds my highest fee,
Films like Titanic,
My greatest hit,
Reservoir Dogs,
My second best.
My boyfriend's Devon Sawa,
My little bit on the side,
I'm really married to the dear Brad Pitt,
Oh isn't it wonderful to have such pride?
Going to the Oscars and the Brits,
BAFTA awards and Grammies,
I've only had twenty nominations,
Nineteen have come through,
I only wish it would come true, if I was . . .

Annaliese Elphick (13)
The Greensward School

FOOTBALL

A football team is made up of eleven men,
If one's sent off, then that leaves ten.
It's played on grass in the shape of a square,
If you were a fan, you'd be sure to be there.

It's made of two halves, at 45 minutes each,
You can play or watch football, or you could even teach.
It's a game that is fast, and also needs skill,
And for players and managers it can be such a thrill.

Each team trains hard and wants to come first,
You need lots of energy, in short and long bursts.
The idea is to score and hit the ball long,
And if a goal comes, the fans sing a song.

The idea is basic, you work as a team,
And if you win trophies, you're considered the cream.
To come top of the league is what teams do strive for,
But if you come bottom, your moral's are on the floor.

When you play you wear shorts, socks and a shirt,
You can play in the rain, the mud and the dirt.
You wear football boots, which helps shield your feet,
Which shields them in tackles when your marker you meet.

In short it's a game, but is serious stuff,
Both player or supporter, you can't get enough.
I love to play, watch, talk, and discuss,
Although Mum will never understand why all the fuss.

She says 'It's only a game, it's only a sport,'
I really think it could be better, if she was taught.
To understand it's more important than life,
And I will make sure in my future,
I find a football crazy wife!

Michael Blaylock (14)
The Greensward School

212

BACK FROM SCHOOL

Getting in from home rushing to get that last chocolate eclair,
Leaving a mess down your school tie,
Which is wiped with a flannel and left over a chair ready to dry,
Slowly walking up the stairs
To the room on the right
Where the sun shines the most.
Now I have to do an essay on the holocaust.
An hour later and all my work is nearly done.
Just in time for dinner,
Where I can sit and watch TV.
After all this I feel a little sleepy,
I crawl up to bed and tuck myself nice and tight,
So all that is left to say is goodnight.

Tom Draper (14)
The Greensward School

TV

Every day I watch TV
Whether it's
Videos,
Films,
Or programmes.
Drama,
Adventure,
Horror too,
I bet I watch it more than you.
One day I'll get square eyes they say,
But that can wait till another day.

Sheryl Wilson (13)
The Greensward School

MOONLIT NIGHT

For the night has come
For the night has gone
Up rises the moon
Down sets the sun
For the day has gone
And the night arisen
The night is dark
As dark as a prison
For the dark moonlight glow
Glows on my window
The moon I look upon
Glows on my pond
And the stars that I like
Sparkle in the night
It is quiet outside
Nothing can be heard
But what's that? Tweet goes a bird
For the morning has come
And the night has gone
No more moonlight on my pond
For the night has gone and so has the moon
But they'll be back
They'll be back soon.

James Young (14)
The Greensward School

MY FIRST DAY AT SCHOOL

I remember my first day at Plumberow School,
The teachers were big and looked so cruel.
I waved goodbye to my mum at the door,
The rest of the day I would see her no more.

We lined up in a straight line to go to assembly,
I sat next to the new friend I made called Emily.
I felt very scared as I walked into the hall,
As there was my headmaster looking at us all.

Soon after that we went out to play,
That was the best part of the day.
We then got taken back into the classroom,
By this time I hoped I could go home soon.

It then started to get better from then on,
We did painting, colouring and sung a song.
We then played on the carpet for a while,
I then began to show a smile.

The bell was rung around midday,
Our teacher was the one who led the way
To the dinner hall where we could eat,
I sat myself down on a seat.

For another hour we had some fun,
Until the afternoon session had begun.
We changed for PE and ran our races,
Some of us had trouble with our laces.

We all packed away ready for story time,
At the end of the day all had turned out fine.
Things have certainly changed today,
Secondary school is all work no play.

Katie Smith (14)
The Greensward School

BREATH

It's closing up,
tighter and tighter,
it's an invisible force.
It slowly takes control.
It's a rope, pulling tighter
growing stronger by the minute.

Then you take the medicine,
it's a saviour,
it kills that force
that rope is cut from round your middle,
and you can breathe again.

The air feels like sweets,
in your lungs.
It's a treat for it to be there.
Soft and fresh, and lots of it,
filling up your lungs.

Jenni Stratford (15)
The Greensward School

THE MAZE OF LIFE

When we are born,
We enter a maze
of problems, joys and
happy days.
We work our way through,
Growing older and wiser,
Then we stop . . .
For we have reached the end,
Oh what a life.

Charlotte Thompson (14)
The Greensward School

I Sense Winter

I want to smell mince pies cooking,
I want to smell the fragrance of the trees,
I want to smell hot fires burning,
I want to smell the freshness of the breeze.

I want to see the snowflakes falling,
I want to see everything covered in snow,
I want to see the birds flying south,
I want to see winter come and summer go.

I want to hear leaves caught in the wind,
I want to hear children playing in the snow.
I want to hear the red robins sing,
I want to hear people going to a Christmas show.

I want to feel cold winds on my face,
I want to feel the frost,
I want to feel the warmth indoors,
I want to feel loved for no cost.

I want to taste the air that I breathe,
I want to taste hot Christmas pud,
I want to taste nothing but cold,
I want to taste whatever I should.

Emma Turnidge (14)
The Greensward School

OLD!

When I'm old and grey I shall dye my hair pillar box red.
Wear clothes brighter than the sun on a hot day,
Buy platform shoes and not fall over,
And I won't care what others think!

I shall set fire alarms off,
Trample on flowers in the public parks,
Stay up all night watching TV and eating chocolate,
And I won't care if I get fat!

I will keep my room as messy as can be,
Roll in mud and get my clothes messy,
Bungee jump off Niagara falls,
And I won't care if I ever smell!

I would buy a brand-new car and try not to crash it,
Listen to loud music,
Stay out partying all night,
And I won't care if I get drunk!

But nowadays I have to be pleased when relatives stay,
Set good examples to my sister,
Work hard at school without messing up,
Keep clean and tidy,
And always smile when there's nothing to smile about.

Maybe I should start being old now,
So people won't be surprised when I suddenly turn old and grey!

Carly West (14)
The Greensward School

I Wonder . . .

I wonder how the birds do fly
And sit upon a branch up high?
I wonder why the tigers roar
And why the big brown bears do snore?
I wonder how it's too cold for snow
And why they put dog's hair in a bow?
I wonder how the sun does rise
And how they put fillings in meat pies?
I wonder where the clouds do go
And why people like Teletubbies Laa-Laa and Po?
I wonder how people can kill and maim
And why they send stuff to 'You've Been Framed'?

All these questions are simple
All these questions are true
But the most puzzling of all is why's the sky blue?

Gemma Smith (14)
The Greensward School

Dogs

Dogs can run around all day,
They're great fun and they love to play.
They run for the ball, you see them go,
They come back too, they're like a yo-yo.
But they have responsibilities as you can tell,
So feed them, love them and care for them well.
And remember well that a dog is for life,
Not just for Christmas.

Sarah Wall (14)
The Greensward School

WHAT CAN I DO?

It's so hard to think of something some days,
Of something to write,
Of something to say.
I mean, where does it come from when there's nothing inside?
And I couldn't think of anything to write if I tried.
But everyone else, they all understand,
They're writing already,
Whereas my pen's not even in my hand.
And how do I concentrate when there's things on my mind,
And there's screams in the hall, as if somebody's died.
If I'm in a test or worse an exam,
And I know, I know the answer,
But my mind gets in a jam.
Sometimes when I'm at a party or just hanging with the guys,
My mind just goes blank and they start to think I'm really shy.
I can be real imaginative, with loads of ideas in my head,
But they turn out really stupid,
So I'll write something else instead.
Why can't people see things from my point of view?
There is nothing to say,
And nothing I can do.

Nicola Frampton (15)
The Greensward School

WAR

The most powerful force
Controlled by madmen
No chance of survival
The killing never stops
The madmen know they're safe
Only the sane watch the mushrooms grow.

Matt Booker (14)
The Greensward School

THE LACE MAKER

She was a lace maker
With bobbins bright and spangled,
She would weave the thread to and fro
And never get entangled.
As time went by her lace would grow
As patterns different she did know.
The pins, they stabbed the pricking fine,
Of brass, they shone and shine
The cotton white it did entwine.
The lace did grow but with much work
It took to finish it.
Then pins came out and bobbins undone,
And check every bit.
She wore no special clothing, 'cept
A cap upon her head.
Her eyes were bright and shining,
As the patterns she did read.
Her fingers told her story, they
Were long and slender too,
The nails had length and dents in
As they put the pins in true.

Rebekah Abrams (14)
The Greensward School

MY FAMILY

My mum and dad split up many years ago,
Which kind of makes life complicated as you'd probably know.
All my grandparents are alive and well,
Although Nan hurt her back the other day when she fell!
My dad has been married twice since my mum,
And my sister, she's alright, just a little dumb.
I have a dog called Jaz, she is family too
I guess so are my other pets, the tortoise, rat and gnu!
I have so many cousins, second cousins as well,
Try squeezing in at Christmas, it is a living Hell!
I will tell you a little more about Mum and Dad,
And my sister, well she is truly mad.
My mum has long brown hair and is a receptionist,
My dad works at a tractor plant, when he is away he's missed.
They actually still got on, which makes life so much easier.
Now my dad lives by the sea where it is more breezier.

Hayley Croft (14)
The Greensward School

CYCLING

C   ycling can keep you very fit.
Y   you can get around without polluting the environment.
C   hildren or adults can take part too.
L   ong or short rides to suit your ability.
I   n to town, to a friend's. Wherever you want to go.
N   ever go out on a bike without a safety helmet on.
G   o on, get out and ride!

Chris Watson (14)
The Greensward School

MY BEST FRIEND

Ten years old and going grey,
He will be faithful, till his dying day.
A rescue dog, that had two broken legs,
These were mended by metal pegs.
He's got the nicest nature,
And never loses his temper.
He sleeps by the side of my bed,
So I can lean down and stroke his head.
When I go out, I never fear,
Because my best friend is always near.
Ben is his name,
Chasing cats is his game.

James Colman (14)
The Greensward School

BASKETBALL

Running with the ball
You feel so very small
Sweating with aggression
Going for the net
Your heart pounding as you aim
You take the shot
You score!
Relief.

John Atkinson (14)
The Greensward School

JUDGEMENT DAY

When the seas boil,
And the land is burning.

When the trees are alight,
And the people are dying.

When people turn to dust before
your eyes,
And thunder and lightning light
the skies.

When the Earth turns to Hell
And demons are unleashed.

When the skies part to reveal a
Throne,
A man and his book will stand
alone.

There and then a man's soul will
be judged
For all the deeds that he has done.

As this day has been named
In history called the judgement day.

Craig Sladden (14)
The Greensward School

LIFE

What is the point of life?
You are born, live for about 80
years, then die.
But it's those 80 years
that are the point of life.
You start by going to school
and
whilst at school you'll have a
group of best mates
who you go out on the town
with
and to the cinema.
You'll have them all your life.
Then you leave school and get a job.
You will meet a man who means the
world to you.
You get married and have 2 or 3 kids
You will still have fun when you are
older
but you will wish you were younger.
Then, your children have
children, and
you find that you are now grandparents.
This is when you feel old.
You sit alone at home as your husband has died
remembering the lovely memories you have.
Then you go for a long sleep
where those memories of life stay with you forever.

Emily Stride (15)
The Greensward School

THE SNOW

Snowflakes falling,
Snowballs flying,
Snowmen sitting,
Snow is fun.

Cats are pouncing,
Cars are stuck,
Dogs are barking,
Snow is fun.

Now the snowflakes are slushy,
Snowballs have landed,
Snowmen have melted,
The snow has gone.

Matthew Sipple (11)
The James Hornsby High School

A MOUSE IN MY HOUSE

I once had a mouse,
  who lived in my house.
I told him to go away,
  but he wanted to stay.
I told him no
  he has to go
But he insisted
  became a bit twisted.
So I called for the cat
  Mouse, he didn't like that!

And left that day.

Gary Fullerton (11)
The James Hornsby High School

MOONO'S MESSAGE

Dear
Michelle
I am an
alien which
you do not know
I come from above
on the Planet Pluto,
I look every day for
my parents somewhere
which planet are they on? I do not care. I've been looking for them
ever since my birth, I've looked over every planet apart from the
Earth. So if you would help me please, oh please, I'm
down on my hands and I'm down on my knees.
I've searched so hard on my spaceship so
small, but wherever I look I see nothing
at all. I almost gave up hope because
nobody cares, I look for my parents
who are always in pairs. Could you
help me because we're the last of our kind,
and I could not put all this sadness
behind.
Yours faithfully
Moono.

Michelle Leonard (11)
The James Hornsby High School

I LAND I . . .

I land, I see
a big, tall thing,
just sitting there.
Not moving.

I hear a noise.
Strange noise
over and over again.

I smell a funny
horrible smell
coming from the
things around me.

I feel nice,
warm and
fresh.

I'm scared,
what are all
the things
all around me.
What should I do?

. . . thought the alien.

Joanne Smith (11)
The James Hornsby High School

THE HOT DOG STAND

I see a massive
big building
in front of my face.

Then a fuzzy
loud noise comes
whistling past my
body.

I smell a lot
of hot-dogs which
smell really good.

A smelly breeze
comes whizzing past
as fast as it
could go.

Now I feel frightened
and really scared
I want to
go home but I
can't go there.

By an alien.

Damion Spencer (11)
The James Hornsby High School

LUCKY PUPPY

Once again I've been thrown across the room.
There is no end
Broken bones
I can hardly move
I'm so fragile
Now I see my chance   *n*
I limp repeatedly
I'm free!
At last
Approaching, sniffing all around
People coming towards me
I hide.
They pick me up
I start crying
They hold me gently
And now I'm relaxed.
After a few years
I realise in the end
I'm a lucky puppy.

Heather Sullivan (11)
The James Hornsby High School

FUN IN THE SUN!

Sun shining
Barbecues lighting,
Children fighting,
Fun in the sun!

Shorts and T shirts,
Old and new shirts,
Green and blue shorts,
Fun in the sun!

Birds singing,
Children winning,
Parents knitting,
Fun in the sun!

Sun has gone,
No more fun,
No shorts or shirts,
No more fun in the sun.

Liam Shorter (11)
The James Hornsby High School

A TOWER

I see a big grey
building just sitting in front
of me.

I hear a loud,
strange fuzzing and
buzzing sound in
my ear.

I smell a horrible
smell like car fumes
in the air.

I feel a slight breeze
against my face.

I feel scared and frightened
nowhere to go
and I want
to go home.

By an alien.

Richard Deadman (11)
The James Hornsby High School

My Mum

My mum
She goes on at me endlessly,
Wash the dishes,
Make the tea,
She is always nagging me.

Hoover here,
Hoover there,
But when I'm sick,
She's always there.

But there you are,
That's my mum,
She's just like my best chum.

Lauren Murphy (12)
Valentines High School

A Poem About My Sister

My sister is a pest
My sister thinks she's the best
My sister and me always get in a fight
My sister always has to be right
My sister makes me mad
My sister's always bad.

But when my sister's not so rude
My sister sometimes cooks me food
I guess my sister is quite cool
My sister isn't so bad after all.

Magaz Idris (13)
Valentines High School

MUM'S SECRET

I thought I knew my mum so well,
Until one night when asleep I fell,
The window smashed,
The door got bashed,
A burglar made his way inside.

My mum awoke straight away,
Dashed like a bullet I would say,
I awoke a little later,
Jumped up like an alligator.

Reached the lounge just in time,
To see my mum beat the crime,
She flipped and spun up in the air,
I couldn't help but shake and stare.

She knocked the gun out of his hand
Then spun around and looked so grand.
She shot and shot,
She shot a lot!

The burglar knew he stood no chance,
In fact he looked like he was in a trance,
He rushed outside holding his butt,
Screaming and shouting like a nut.

My mum just smiled, laughed and said,
'Come on Tom, back to bed.'

Thomas Cheam (12)
Valentines High School

FLYING ERNIE

There was a lonely parrot
The parrot lived in a cage
The parrot was called Ernie
He goes a long journey.

(Refrain)

Ernie, Oh Ernie
Why do you try to escape?
You're my pal, I'll find you a gal
Please stay, don't escape.

The owner of the parrot
Had his pay
The owner took Ernie out
And started dancing about.

(Refrain)

The owner put Ernie back
Ernie got the catch
That he forgot to hatch the latch
Ernie tried to open the beige cage.

(Refrain)

Ernie escaped
Through the window he went
He bent through pipes
And went high as the kites.

(Refrain)

As the days went on
So did Ernie
As he ended up in Jamaica
People wanted to bake him!

(Refrain)

The people caught Ernie
This time he didn't escape
They threw an arrow at him
And laughed at him.

(Refrain)

Ernie, Oh Ernie
Why did you escape?
You know I took good care of you
Ernie, Oh Ernie why did you escape?

Mariam Khan (13)
Valentines High School

MY GRANDMA

Grandma, Grandma,
Gives to me,
Chocolate pudding
And hot sweet tea.

She sits up high,
On her rocking chair.
She can't touch the floor,
But she doesn't care.

Grandma, Grandma,
Is tiny and grey
I wonder if,
She'll shrink away.

Grandma, Grandma,
Has wrinkled skin.
Her glasses lean,
And I'm the next of kin.

Lena Doshi (12)
Valentines High School

LITTLE MIRACLES

I saw the baby on the television set,
it grinned at me, I stared back.
I doodled aimlessly on a piece of paper
I looked at the baby again
Then it occurred to me that
every single minute, every hour, every day
a baby is born somewhere in our world.
A fresh face, a new life, a new soul.
comes as a blessing for some
and a nightmare for others.
Little eyes, little nose, little mouth.
A fragile small person that will mature and become stronger.
Small eyes, small hands, small feet.
A tiny new being that will grow and become an adult
and then
it won't be a little miracle anymore.

Harsha Patel (14)
Valentines High School

OSMAN

Osman's face is really long,
His eyes are small and narrow
His spotty face, his spiky hair,
And plus his teeth are yellow.

He pulls me out of my chair,
And kicks me down the stairs
He makes me want to pull out my hair,
He also gives me a bit of a scare!

A really big scare!

Sundeep Singh Athwal (12)
Valentines High School

THE ICE-CREAM MAN

There once lived an ice-cream man,
Who drove through Raspberry Land,
He drove and drove, he sold and sold,
Until he was king of the land.

The town's people were not impressed,
But the children thought they were blessed,
He drove and drove, he sold and sold,
Until he was king of the land.

He now drove from town to town,
All before the sun went down,
He drove and drove, he sold and sold,
Until he was king of the land.

But then one day he failed to come,
At this time I was with my mum
He drove and drove, he sold and sold,
Until he was king of the land.

This was when I came into the story,
I came in with great glory,
He drove and drove, he sold and sold,
Until he was king of the land.

I then walked up to his house
Where I saw a great big mouse,
He drove and drove, he sold and sold,
Until he was king of the land.

Finally I walked up to his bed,
And in my surprise, I found him dead,
He drove and drove, he sold and sold,
Until he was king of the land.

Komal Ghai (13)
Valentines High School

THE HAUNTED HOUSE

Once there were ten girls going on a rip.
It was to a big old house.
When they got there,
Jane saw a dead old mouse.
Nights to remember

It was time to go to sleep,
I was knocked off my feet.
I woke up early, told my friends
Where to meet.
Nights to remember

We all explored the house
We went to eat
In the old kitchen
I was cold, so were my feet
Nights to remember

The day went fast
It was time to go to sleep
It was freezing cold
The mountains were steep
Nights to remember

The tapping on the windows made me scared
I was feeling alone
The girls were out exploring the place
The morning had gone the sunlight shone
Nights to remember

It started to rain
I was ready to leave.
It had been horrible
I had to believe.
Nights to remember.

Samerah Yasin (12)
Valentines High School

MY BIRTHDAY

Today's my birthday party
And I just can't wait
I'm really very happy
Today I've just turned eight.

This morning I woke up
My mum and dad gave me lots of presents
I got a doll, toy car and a new dress too.
Today I've just turned eight.

I helped my mum prepare the food
Crisps, drinks and pepperoni sandwiches.
I couldn't wait
Today I've just turned eight.

The cake had been prepared and decorated with sweets,
It was really big
I couldn't wait
Today I've just turned eight.

The party was over
I was happy no more.
I had a pile of presents all around me
Today I've just turned eight.

Tayeba Mobeen (12)
Valentines High School

MISTLETOE MOUNTAIN

I went on a trip far far away
I went to Mistletoe Mountain.
It had a large and empty garden
with a rusty and empty fountain.

I'd heard about some buried gold
I don't really believe it.
Though that's what I was told.

I didn't care about the silly tales
my friend told me there was a ghost.
But a haunted house *ha, ha, ha!*
That must have been a hoax.

Though when I was sleeping
Late into the night.
I had heard a loud noise
I woke with such a fright.

I decided to take a stroll
and have a look around.
And then I saw some movement
I had heard a weird sound.

The ghost had finally come
it's come to take me away.
It took me to a cellar,
it left me there, for a year and a day.

I write this so you know
what happened here to me.
I'm telling you this within my sorrow
I am going to die here tomorrow.

But hey at least I lived my life
I'm telling you never to snoop around.
Don't worry about the nightly sound
And that was the story of mistletoe mountain . . .

Audrey Hodge (13)
Valentines High School

MY FIRST DAY AT SCHOOL

It's my first day at school
I'm really excited, I can't wait
I'm gonna make new friends
I really just can't wait.

I finally arrived at school
Everyone was looking at me and laughing
I saw my new teacher and
My teacher said, 'Hi,' to me, and the kids

I had my first subject at school
And I loved it because we sat around
We had lots of fun and we played
It was nearly time to go home

We played as much as we could but
The teacher said, 'Come in now. Pack away and sit.'
So we had to go and say, 'Bye,' to our teacher and
Our teacher said, 'Bye,' to us.

Yashna Solanki (12)
Valentines High School

FOOTBALL MANIAC

There was a boy called Tom
He was always in a state,
He really liked football,
And he played for Year 8.

He wanted to play for a team,
He thought of Man Utd
He went to go for trials
But he was short-sighted.

So he signed up for trials,
And he went to play,
He played a practice match,
But he had nothing to say.

He waited for the answer,
And the letter came,
The answer was yes,
And they said he was best.

Shabeer Dean (12)
Valentines High School

CRUNCHIE

Get up Crunchie you're dreaming again.
You're not Gunger Din
You're not Robin Hood
You're not a brave knight
Or a king that's been crowned.
You're just plain old Crunchie . . . the howling hound.

Nabeel Raja (12)
Valentines High School

THE TITANIC CREW

The night is cool
The sky is blue
The Titanic Ship is sailing through
Beware you crew it could be you.

The crew is dancing
The time is ticking
The Titanic Ship is stunning
Beware you crew it could be you.

The sailors see
A big ice treat
Oh no they shout
Beware you crew it could be you.

People frowning
People rowing
People think 'Let's go and hurry'
Beware you crew it could be you.

People shouting
People counting
People see the big ice mounting
Beware you crew it could be you.

Everyone's worried
Everyone's sorry
Everyone's crying for luck and vote
Beware you crew it could be you.

That's all
The time is up
Bye, bye everyone
Beware you crew it is *you*.

Randeep Khela (12)
Valentines High School

THE SIMPSONS VS THE FLANDERS

'Twas a stormy night down
In Springfield, two families stood in woe
They cursed each other day and night
They always swore at each other in woe
But then something happened

Their children left them
Because of their disgrace to
Each other as they were always fighting
They went in search of their children
But they kept on fighting

They searched and searched
But they kept on fighting
And all the time their children were
Heading towards Chicago
But Flanders and Simpsons kept on fighting

They were fighting during the day
They were fighting during the night
They never got closer to finding
Their children
But they kept on fighting

Ten days passed but their children
Were never found
But they drove and drove
But they kept on fighting

But then one day they found them
And took them back to Springfield
But a miracle happened
The Simpsons and Flanders
Were fighting no more.

Graham Fairbrother (12)
Valentines High School

THE UNLUCKIEST MAN EVER

There was a man named Tim
who was an unlucky man.
No one really liked him
he was so unlucky.

He had a real good job
but he heard he'd been fired.
He then began to sob
he was so unlucky.

He went home to his wife
to tell her his bad news.
He'd found she'd left his life
he was so unlucky.

Then poor Tim lost his house
they took his wealth as well.
All he had was his little mouse
he was so unlucky.

Then he was put in jail
there was no reason why.
He couldn't pay the bail
he was so unlucky . . .

Nicholas Illman (13)
Valentines High School

ROLLER-COASTERRIFIC

The first time I ever went on a roller-coaster,
was when I was eleven years old.
I was in a Theme Park and I saw the Vortex
it was great - or so I was told!

The first time I ever went on a roller-coaster,
I was queuing up in the line.
I got to the front and I sat in the seat
and I knew I was gonna be fine.

The first time I ever went on a roller-coaster.
we were moving up the track.
Up and up I went, I was so scared,
and I wished I could just go back.

The first time I ever went on a roller-coaster.,
We went zooming down the hill.
It went upside down, and I screamed so loud
I thought I was gonna be ill.

The first time I ever went on a roller-coaster,
it was the best ride I'd been on.
I wanted to go on it again and again,
but before I could ask the others had gone!

Aisha Ali (12)
Valentines High School

I Want To Be A Pop star

I want to be a pop star
the best there could ever be.
The only person who doubts me is my pa
I'll show him, never to mess with me.

I want to be a pop star
I wanted to sing about the sea.
We wrote a song, just me any my ma
She didn't charge me, it was free.

I want to be a pop star
I sang my song just after tea.
It was very good, I should go far.
They heard my song, and paid me a fee.

I want to be a pop star
I want everyone to see.
I went to a bar
I sung my song! It was meant to be.

I want to be a pop star
everyone hear my plea.
I think I'm now a star
Hey! Look on *Top of the Pops*- it's me . . .

Saba Akram (13)
Valentines High School

BLACKPOOL THRILLS

The day I went to Blackpool,
I was so excited, especially,
when I was told I'd get the day off school.
I started to shout hooray! Hooray!

The day I went to Blackpool,
we parked next to the Pepsi-Max.
Then my dad started to play the fool,
saying 'Baby-ride, baby-ride!'

The day I went to Blackpool,
I was getting really hungry.
So I decided to be cruel,
and I scoffed up all the food.

The day I went to Blackpool,
I was forced to go on the Pepsi-max.
I thought it would be cool,
but oh my God, how I screamed!

The day I went to Blackpool,
I had so much fun.
Then I saw a ghoul . . .
and I screamed all the way home.

Vinisha Saund (12)
Valentines High School

SOMETHING THAT MAKES ME THINK

It was early in the morning,
when the paper came through the post.
The headline was bad enough
but page four was even worse.

I was reading the news on page four
it was shocking and extremely sad.
Not only was I stunned
but also my mum and dad.

Why did he have to die mum?
He was only a little boy,
he had his life yet to live
and also to enjoy.

'Now that he has gone, mum
I bet they're really sad.
Especially all his relatives
and also his mum and dad.'

'Let him rest in peace, mum
and remember him for the good.
Let him fly like an angel,
like he always wanted to.'

Tina Bhatia (14)
Valentines High School

ALL SIXTEEN GONE

It took me a while
to figure it out.
What they were talking about
but then I realised.

I didn't know what I felt
Upset, sad, frozen.
I just froze
Thoughts ran across my mind.

Who?
I thought.
Who would do such a thing?
Who would have the nerve?
To face those innocent children
And hold up his gun
Bang!

All 16 gone . . .

Why?
Why would they do such a thing?
Then turned towards the teacher.
Then
Himself!

Pavendeep Virk (14)
Valentines High School

DEATH

Everything's fine for a moment
but then when you find out.
Your life seems to go downhill
all you want to do
is scream and shout.

You don't think
you can't stand any more.
You need to lie down
it all seems unreal
but you know no one's clowning around.

Something like this when it happens
really breaks your heart.
You know you've got to deal with it
but you don't know how to start.

How can we stop the pain?
It will never go away,
I'll stay with us forever.
Well, until we fade away.

I'm told we have to get on with our lives
we can't cry forever.
He's gone now - deal with it!
You'll never see him again -
Ever . . . !

Jaspreet Matharu (14)
Valentines High School

THE AWAKENING

I came downstairs,
switched on the television.
News was on Channel 1.
2
Then 3
Then 4
Lastly 5
All I saw was news.

I switched it off
not knowing it was about her.
Wondering why the news was on
all the channels.
It bothered me, not knowing
why
so I turned it onto Channel 1.

They were talking about a women
in a car accident.
I thought it was just anyone
I didn't know it was her!

I listened carefully and then paused.
I realised who it was.
Shocked, startled, I couldn't believe it
now I knew why
the news was on every channel.

They said she died in Paris
at about 4.00 am in the morning.
On Sunday 31st August 1997.

The news shocked the nation
and people gathered to mourn.
They'll never forget
the good she did
to help the sick and poor.

It taught me a thing or two
about what life can do to you.
Live life to the full
as every minute counts.

Aqila Khan (15)
Valentines High School

JIM THE TROUBLED PUPIL

There was once a boy called Jim
He stands at the school gate.
I don't want to write his story
But what can I do, I'm his mate?

He stands at the gate
Waits for a little boy
Then bashes him up
Like treating a toy.

He gets work set by the teacher
He throws it in the bin.
The teacher shouts at him
He pops the teacher's stomach with a pin!

As Jim is a troubled pupil
What's going to happen to him now?
He knows he's going to get suspended
He thinks, 'No more school. Wow!'

Ravinder Pahngli (12)
Valentines High School

UNDER PRESSURE

It's piling up
more and more.
Homework,
more homework!

As I sit down to start one piece,
I remember
there's another three pieces to do.

I sit alone
to think about what to write.
But all I can hear is
GCSE's, Exams, A's and B's course work
Exams, A's and B's course work
filling my head.

Thoughts and feelings enter my head
If I do
If I don't
What will the consequences be?

I must do my best
Year 10
What a mess!

GCSE's, Exams A's and B's course work
Exams, A's and B's GCSE's course work.

Homework, homework
higher and higher.
It's piling up.

I must do my best . . .
What a mess!

Kerri Bywater (14)
Valentines High School

MY BALLAD

My name is Kiran Khalid
I go to Valentines High
It's sometimes boring
because everybody likes to sigh.

I came to school late
I was feeling sick.
I was late when I entered my classroom
my teacher gave me a tick.

I went to my lessons
but forgot my homework.
I did it during my lessons
then I realised I forgot my book.

I got in trouble for wearing white trainers.
The teacher gave me a detention.
I wasn't feeling well at all
I wasn't paying attention.

Finally, I was going home
I couldn't wait
I was in trouble again . . .
My mother asked me 'Why are you so late?'

Kiran Khalid (12)
Valentines High School

THE CHILDREN'S REVENGE!

There was an old and mean man
A man who hated children
The man was rich and mad
And had a house as big as a building.

There was an old and mean man
The children would play on his land
The man was rich and mad
They would play until they were sad.

There was an old and mean man
Who would laugh at their pity
The man was rich and mad
They would kill every kitty.

There was an old and mean man
The children decided to pay him back
The man was rich and mad
The children tried to tie him up in a sack.

There was an old and mean man
The children tried to open his window with a stick
The man was rich and mad
But instead smashed it with a great heavy brick.

There was an old and mean man
The children then broke in.
The man was rich and mad
But fell over some tins.

There was an old mean man
Who had a huge fright
The man was rich and mad
And later died at night.

Nosheen Aslam (12)
Valentines High School

256

MY TRIP TO OXFORD

The first time I went to Oxford
I was very happy with glee
I had so much fun
And it was very me . . .

The first time I went to Oxford
In the month of May
From morning to evening
It was only for a day . . .

The first time I went to Oxford
I went by train from home.
Then took a coach and approached Oxford
And it was very close . . .

The first time I went to Oxford
I went to a museum
And went shopping
And it was fun . . .

The first time I went to Oxford
Had McDonalds
I sat on a tour bus
And it was very depriving . . .

Sadia Mehmood (13)
Valentines High School

YEAR EIGHT

My name is Sonal Patel
I'm always in a state
this is my sad story
I don't have much fun in Year 8.

My name is Sonal Patel
and I don't have much fun.
I'm happy with my teacher
there's not much I have done.

My name is Sonal Patel
I don't have much to say
It's a big problem
that's why I stay away.

My name is Sonal Patel
I have a lot of foes.
Their names are Gemma and Emma
so don't take the mickey out of my nose.

My name is Sonal Patel
that's what I've been told.
So far it's been there for 12 years
I know I'm getting old.

Sonal Patel (13)
Valentines High School

THE MAN FROM CHINA

There once was a man from China
Who wasn't a very good climber.
And whilst he was visiting France
He made up this really weird dance.

He jumped up and down
People said 'He's a clown!'
When they went to bed
A man had lost his head.

You know this man from China
Who wasn't a very good climber.
He was very fat
He looked like a dumb-bat.

He told everyone he met
That he had made this bet
That he was going to climb the
Leaning tower of Pisa.

As he got to the top
There was this very loud pop.
And with such a groan
And a big loud moan

The leaning tower of Pisa fell.
And all that was left of the man from China
Was this great big splodge
Looking like a great blodge.

So he was wasted
And he was done . . .
And now this horrible tale is done!

Rowland Peck (12)
Valentines High School

DEATH OF BILLY

It was sad that day
the sun was really gleaming.
The driver went on
and the train was really steaming.

Billy Jones was his name
he had all sorts of fame.
Said goodbye to his family
and off to work again.

The journey was really long
he knew something was wrong.
He didn't know, he scratched his head
Oh no! A train coming ahead . . .

The train went on another 50
and on another 5.
The train crashed up ahead
he was surely dead not alive.

But when the paramedics came
they thought he was dead.
At last they found him *hurrah, hurrah*
But could not find his head . . .

Jason Triphook (12)
Valentines High School

HORROR HOUSE

We were out in the dead of night
and we all had a fright.
It was a dark, dark, night
and all was still.

We saw the house
and a giant mouse.
It was a dark, dark, night
and all was still.

It enticed us near
and we started to fear.
It was a dark, dark, night
and all was still.

We entered the villa
and we saw the killer.
It was a dark, dark, night
and all was still.

She took her knife
and she took a life.
It was a dark, dark, night
and all was still.

We ran and ran
and we saw our Nan.
It was a dark, dark, night
and all was still.

It was a heavenly sight
and boy did the killer have a fright.
It was a dark, dark, night
and all was still.

Emma Riley (12)
Valentines High School

BEES

I came downstairs
there were bees on my breakfast.
Bees on my nose
Bees in my school bag
I shouted 'Oh not bees again
I hope it does not stay the same.'

I went in the car
there were bees
in my ear hole.
Bees in my shoe sole.
I shouted 'Oh not bees again
I hope it does not stay the same.'

I went in my classroom
there were bees in my books.
Bees on my looks
'Oh, not bees in my books.
I have to give it to Mrs Hooks!'

I went to lunch
there were bees in my packed lunch.
Bees in a big bunch
Bees going munch, munch.
'Oh, not bees again
I hope it does not stay the same!'

I was on the way home
I was all alone.
There were bees up ahead
Bees in my head.
'Oh, not bees again
I hope I drop down dead . . .'

Rohit Sharma (12)
Valentines High School

ADVENTURE ISLAND

The giant gates swing open
like a fortress hailing the conquering army;
They've come by car, bus and train,
to experience the wonders and sensations
of this magical world.

People are hurled from side to side
as if they were on a boat during a hard storm.
The sounds of their screams echoing for miles around.
The smell of hot dogs draw them to the stand,
like lions being pulled to their prey.

The splashes of the rides make tidal waves six feet tall.
Like a storm whipping the sea;
The slot machines flash and clink,
Attracting human flies to their spider's web.
At night the lights and noises thunder across the park,
as if at a high profile sporting event.

As evening turns to night the park sleeps.
The rides taking on the shapes of giants.
The wind blowing spookily through them,
as they speak to each other secretively.
The only other sound is the sea
gently lapping the coast.
Finally the sun rises and the park returns
to its festive atmosphere.

Dominic Charles (12)
Westcliff High School for Boys

THE PRITTLE BROOK

As I sit at the side
of the old Prittle Brook.
I watch the water trickle
through its carved concrete path.
Like the steady flow of traffic
on the A127.   *

I sit on the bank
the hospital looming over me
and towering over Prittlewell High.
Over-shadowing the place where I sit
like a huge fortress.
Full of instruments that
flash and bleep and
blink frantically
as if in a panic.

The water that I watch
sitting on the bank
is brown with mud
dirt and grime.
Bits of rubbish float in its clutches
being thrashed and
rolled about the place.
Debris like cans, bags and bits of wood
even a broken car windscreen and a dead bird!

And so
as the hands of time turn to 5 o'clock.
I begin my journey home.
Leaving behind
the trickling water
and the ever-looming
ever-towering
fortress . . .

Richard Piccone (13)
Westcliff High School for Boys

A WALK IN THE WOODS

In the ancient woodland at Hadleigh
the daylight peers through the canopy of trees.
Like a radioactive liquid in cracks in a wall.
The chatter of chirping from the birds
sound like an orchestra warming up.
And the scattered army of trees stands
as straight as an assortment of telegraph poles.
They seem to have stepped closer together
thickening as they get further away.
Like water-colours running together.
The fresh smell of grass creeps into my senses
like a cat slinking towards a goldfish bowl.
The rustle of leaves and snapping of twigs beneath my feet
are like stationery being crushed in a crusher bin.
The tight sagging bark around the old trees
feels like the skin on a shrunken head.
The crisp air of the autumn morning
has a taste of sweet, cold, candy ice-cubes.
The yells and shrieks from the chipmunk children
sound like bells far away in the distance.

Matthew Wilson (12)
Westcliff High School for Boys

Your Messages For Today

I left you my dreams on an answer machine
All my hope and despair inside me.
Mixed-up emotions ruling me.
Through my dreams which only I can see
Never repeated, remembered or chosen.
All living in my subconscious mind
Ruling my sleep.
So many voices.
Thoughts and imagination.
I'm a million different people
From one minute to the next.
All my dreams
So different yet seem so real.
I see it through my darkest days.
Keep catching the butterfly
In that dream of mine.
In a dreamy wilderness I am restless
Escaping for a new identity.

Adam Grant (15)
Westcliff High School for Boys

The Black Forest, Germany

Quiet, as quiet as an empty room;
Only the noise of the engine disturbing the silence.
The road, twisting and climbing
like a snake.

Hear . . .
the roar of the waterfall in your ear.
Let your mind run free,
as free as a bird,
aromatic Black Forest air
in the nostrils.

Glistening powder snow, gleaming in the sun.
Children having fun.
Fir trees, mountain skyline,
magical walking through the forest.

Feel the tingle of the air on your skin
Silence, peace and stillness;
Dreams one cannot forget . . .

Michael Burstin (12)
Westcliff High School for Boys

Upon A Calm Mountain

The Laurentian Mountains in Canada in the early morning
Are as still as an empty room.
Standing on the side of the mountain I can see for miles around.
The pine trees are javelins thrown from the top of the mountain.
The lake is a sheet of metal with a bright light shining off it -
Untouched and unbroken.
The morning diamond dew on the grass sparkles
While the choir of birds is singing a happy morning tune
As they awake.

With no one around it is as if I am the last person on the face of the
                                                earth.
As I breathe in my first few breaths it freshens my mouth like mint
                                                toothpaste.
Where I am standing the grass is a luscious green,
And further away it looks aquamarine.
As the wind hits the trees I begin to feel cold.
Looking down at the village the houses only seem big enough for ants.
The roofs are bright green and red
Like Christmas decorations.

Oliver Marcus (12)
Westcliff High School for Boys

THE PALACE THEATRE GREEN ROOM

As I arrive
I smell the smoke of cigarettes wafting slowly upwards.
I see the walls, as pink as the early morning sun, flash out to me.
I sit down on the old tatty sofa.
Waiting for the actors to arrive.

As they approach
I hear them come in a wave of noise.
The steam-train of noise and hubbub.
The noise of their singing and laughing consumes the room.
But it all goes silent as a voice over the tannoy says:
'This is your fifteen minute call.'
As quickly as they have come - they leave.
An army of thespians
Now it's all quiet and the show begins.

As I stand up
just about to walk across the browning carpet.
An actor arrives, and I get entangled in his interesting
conversation on how someone messed up on stage.
Or how their business is booming:
I get the feeling of boredom as he rambles on.
Then my friend arrives
and we quickly make our way to our dressing room.
We've got to get changed:
We're on soon . . .

William Crow (13)
Westcliff High School for Boys

ANOTHER TRIP TO MY NIGHTMARE

Thorpe Bay Station shrouded in darkness.
Wintry cold on this night.
The rustling leaves blow along the ground,
Tree branches fighting as they were joined by the gales.
The roughness of the tree feels
Like an old man's wrinkled brow.
The coldness shivers up me, seated on a rigid metal seat
Waiting . . .
The old haunted house next to the station bleakly looking down
As if it is watching me through the darkness.
The hooting of the owl from the tree
Brings out the goose-bumps in me.
Ghostly sounds in the distance, laughing, screaming out.
The ants attacking when tormented by my stamping.
A dank, damp smell passes through my nose.
From the shadow - can it be! The outline of the train.
Late again . . .
Approaching the station with caution.
A screeching witch being burnt at the stake.
The coloured metal boxes appearing and disappearing
every now and then;
Slamming doors echoing everywhere;
And my mum appearing like a super-hero through the mist
She's home . . .

Jon Brown (12)
Westcliff High School for Boys

THE LAZY LAWN

Sitting in the garden
on the cloud-soft grass.
With the heat on my skin.
Gentle breeze.

Huge trees slowly sway
birds come to quench their thirst.
Tabby-cat crouches, not to be seen.
Dancing craneflies.

Peace becomes a part of me,
lazily watch a ballerina bee.
Butterflies flying towards violent red roses,
trapped in a pot.

Colours fizz together,
eyes begin to close.
Gentle sleep.

Slowly begin to stir,
just a dream, for outside there's a muddy lawn.
I wish for the dream to be true.

Michael Johnson (13)
Westcliff High School for Boys

NEVER-ENDING FLAME

I remember well that dark looming day:
Stripped so quickly from my life, gone forever.
Now a black memory of pain and anguish.
How could it happen? Why did it happen?
No longer does the wondrous steam of life
flow with such elegant grace.
So unexpected, so unannounced.
Left in misery for all of time.
Her flame of life went out so quickly, extinguished.
Always a part of me, an empty void.
My life left discarded, superfluous,
no longer does the earth bear the power of being.
The end of life and existence which is
so shrouded in mystery and fear.

I am left naive and wondering where
a spirit so strong and eternal
can have gone - discarded? Will I ever know?
What will my life be like without her being?
How can I progress without her guidance?
Now the earth has claimed her soul forever.
Will I ever know her again? Who will know?
I only wish that I could say good-bye,
to pray that I could see her once again
and say how much I treasured her in life.
To say how much I miss her now she's gone.
If I could only see her once again,
but she has gone forever and I cannot say.
How much I'll always love her
And how much I miss her today.

Luke Meadows (15)
Westcliff High School for Boys

THE WONDERS OF NATURE

Listen to the soft wind
Breathing through the grass.
It seems so calm and gentle
Like waves lapping on the shore.

It is not as gently as it seems,
To little insects - it's a whirlwind.
A hurricane, a tornado, a tempest,
Scattering them in its wake.

The wispy cirrus clouds are my favourites
I sometimes wonder how high they are!
They seem like icing on a cake
You can almost taste the sweetness.

The wind is ageless - it travels far
To the land of the rising sun:
An optical illusion some might say
As it chases rainbows across the sky.

I'd love to see a volcano erupt
Molten magma spewing ever upwards.
Clouds of black ash spreading
Blown ever outward throughout the land.

Boiling rocks crash to the ground
Causing havoc to all in their path.
The lava spreads and flows with speed.
A river causing devastation.

Mother Nature we must remember,
Gives us life as well as death;
We must take the good, embrace it
But accept the bad with grace.

Alan S Klein (11)
Westcliff High School for Boys

SANDY SHORES

The promenade unrolled like an endless carpet,
stained and gum-splattered it lies.
People come and go moving like soldier ants.
In a skyline monotone lies a sunset radiant in beauty.
A battered loom of pebbles plays a ghostly tune.

I keep on walking . . .

Kiosks stand ever serving sticky confectionery and cold fluids.
The sand weaves between my toes.
Ticklingly annoying but pleasurable.
I like this place, a place of joy and sticky summer sunsets.

I keep on walking . . .

A familiar scent wafts through the air.
Sea creatures scurry in man-made buckets of acid,
The giants then take them up slipping in and devouring.
The sea reflects a pure complexion of torn colours looming above.

I stop . . .

I take it in:
A relaxed finish to a walk on the shady shores.

Roman Prejbisz (12)
Westcliff High School for Boys

THE ESSENCE OF LAKE MEADOWS PARK

As you walk towards my local park,
You can hear the shrill cries of children playing on the swings.
Like weak puppies squealing for their first milk.
The old leaves on the swaying trees hang sad and perishable.
Waiting for the inevitable time for them to helplessly glide,
Down into the ferocious jaws of the spiky grass.

As you walk into the centre of the park.
You can see the proud, commanding lake,
smiling at you through the sun's reflection.
Isolated and desolate stands a feeble island in the middle.
Cowardly sitting there doing nothing except,
For the occasional wave of a tree to a passing visitor.

In a distant field a small space is occupied by two thin white posts.
Standing neglected and sad as two young school boys,
Create their own goal out of jumpers, anoraks and bags.

As autumn has arrived the path leading out of the park
is like a patchwork quilt.
Of reds and golds from the discouraged leaves,
Lying there distressed and defeated from the strength
of the ever-conquering wind.
Knowing that their life shall soon end up in extinction.

Sam J Irwin (12)
Westcliff High School for Boys

THE SHIPWRECK OF MY ROOM

My room is the scene of a shipwreck,
The carpet slowly being covered by a creeping tide of debris,
The flotsam and jetsam of my daily life
Scattered across the floor.

My desk is littered with books
And useless pieces of paper,
And in the thick of it all
Is my doodled English essay.

Yet when I return to the comfort of my bed
I still find no peace,
The deafening waves of sound from my ghetto-blaster
Crashing upon my ears,
And the blaring of the TV,
Keeping me awake all night.

And in the corner of my room
My repulsive dirty washing basket,
As if it was a giant deranged octopus,
With odorous tentacles of socks
Escaping from this nauseating beast of the sea,
Exhaling an odour so great
It could drive a man mad.

This is my shipwrecked room:
Enter . . . if you dare!

Adam Hart (12)
Westcliff High School for Boys

THE STORM

The humid suffocating atmosphere of a summer's day on the
                                    Mediterranean,
Crowds of people on the beach,
But in the space of a few minutes, the sky became a curtain of darkness,
From the sea Poseidon's mighty hand arose covering the land in a dense
                                    rain storm,
Then the heaven's opened and from them came mighty thunder and
                                    lightning,
A huge gale making the palm trees wave in the wind like a rock concert
                                    audience.
The sand was no longer a ghostly white but a fiery storm of gold,
The smell of sea salt in the air,
Only the cathedral standing out mountain-like on the Spanish plains
                                    stood its ground.
The hounding of the savage storm continued throughout the night but
                                    died before dawn,
And tomorrow brings - no evidence of yesterday's storm.

Edward Sluys (12)
Westcliff High School for Boys

BEMBRIDGE BEACH

The sea at Bembridge is like a mirror;
If you throw a stone at it, it cracks and that's bad luck.
Travelling along the mirror are triangular boats
with silk sails blowing gently in the wind.
On the beach is seaweed
it's hands holding onto shells.
Black and slimy it slithers through your own hands,
like a snake slithering over its prey.

Yellow is the sand - like freshly buttered toast;
crunch and creak goes the sand as you walk on it.
The sand goes in between your toes and tickles your feet.
You must watch your feet; the crabs pop up from nowhere!
The crabs are orange ovals with long stick-like legs
and their pincers are like razors.
From up on the cliffs you can
hear the noisy chatter of the people
and you can smell the food from the pub,
all warm and sweet-smelling . . .

Richard Day (12)
Westcliff High School for Boys

OLD LEIGH

The wall of wind stings my cheeks as I sit on the wharf,
watching the hand of the waves clawing at the sea wall.
It is a far cry from the monster arcade machines
and the UFO flashing street lights of Southend.
The swarm of water-borne fishing vessels
chug at snail's pace,
like old traction engines,
along the creek.
They return from their fishing harvest,
gathering in a spaghetti junction of nets,
loaded with rewards of their day's fishing.
I walk down to the desert beach,
now empty as night falls.
Shells like broken porcelain are scattered randomly across the sands.
I look out to sea:
The estuary has gone to sleep,
and become a tranquil haven of peace.

Robert Grover (12)
Westcliff High School for Boys

AFTER THE BELL RINGS

A scramble for the door.
A push and a shove.
The struggling meleé
is forced into the street.

Running to the bus stop
shuffling down the road.
Angry shouts and cackling laughter
of children going home.

The scramble for the bus door
of those anxious to get home.
The looks of disgust
of those who stand aloof.

Children rush out of bus doors,
and onto dirty pavements.
Rushing quickly to their own front door
shouted farewells as friends part.

And suddenly the streets fall silent
like a desolate ghost town.
Birds begin to sing again.
Cats look out from holes
and normality returns . . .

Mark Amos (13)
Westcliff High School for Boys

DEATH BED

The child watched his father fading away.
He felt his pain;
He winced at each of his strained movements:
Once healthy and strong, now withered and grey.

He had known it would happen.
But, why now? Could it not come another day?
It was like an evil spirit -
Could it not take someone else?
He would be good forever:
He promised with all his heart.

Could his father not be given a second chance?
Why did he have to rot away?
What could he do to arouse him
From his terrible peaceless sleep?

He remembered the anger he had felt.
How on his knees he had cursed and shaken his father's arm;
Why was he deserting him so soon?

He cried.
They told him to dry his tears.
'It's not what he would have wanted,' they said.

Mark Crow (15)
Westcliff High School for Boys

THE FRY-UP

As I walk through the door
there is a distinctive smell of
sizzling fat, hot fish and meat pies as well.
Behind the counter the staff
are scampering like squirrels
to serve the food on time.
Salt, vinegar and ketchup
soldiers standing to attention
armed and ready
to advance on the food.
Shiny bright tiles
as green as lime can be:
I don't know whether they are meant to be
. . . attractive,
But to me they look old fashioned and dull.
Chips, crisp and luscious
wrapped in paper white,
like caterpillars
wrapped in their cocoons.
As I go home in the car
the smell lingers and clings to my clothes
like bark to a tree.

Matthew Apps (13)
Westcliff High School for Boys

NEXT

The rain and wind come down
To take their next victim.
While the trees stand their ground
Though they know that they will be overwhelmed
By the rain and wind's strength.
As the road signs hold their defensive positions,
They must wonder if the battle's lost or won.
As the ranks of flowers are crushed by the wind
And shattered by the rain's bullets;
They must wonder -
Who's next?

As the howling wind flies through the air
It hears the crackle of the neighbour's barbecue.
The wind shoots down as quick as lightning
Towards the barbecue
And all that is left is
The putrid smell of smoke.
As the rain shoots down
It volleys a shower of bullets over the people's homes,
Their roofs begin to crumble and change from
A benevolent brown to a consuming black.
Insects are frightened as they try to find a way
Into the people's homes because they couldn't
Help wondering -
Who's next?

Saif Abed (12)
Westcliff High School for Boys

MY ROOM

My room is my little haven,
when I want to be by myself.
I close the door and shut out all sounds.
I turn on my stereo so I don't feel totally alone,
then relax in my carousel chair.

My desk is untidy:
Pens, pencils, paper are strewn about.
The shelves are weighed down
with books standing up like soldiers out of line.

My feet feel the tenderness of the carpet;
it is a great vastness of blue.
Blue is ordinarily cold,
but this room is warm,
and I feel a red glow inside.

I spin round in my chair,
which sighs with relief as I get up to go,
and climb the stairs to my mountain in the sky.
My bed is an inverted four poster,
once in bed I feel like I am floating on air.

The pillows are soft, as I snuggle up and sleep.

Mark McGregor (12)
Westcliff High School for Boys

THE GARDEN

I walk out into my garden
In the early morning sun.
It floats high up in the sky, a large yellow balloon.
Hear the birds singing like a choir
Whistling, laughing, calling to each other.
The trees bend from side to side,
The wind blows their long green tentacles
Like octopuses dancing in the sea.
The morning dew glistens on the grass
Round my footprints behind me.
The flowers burst into life
The colours so vivid, so bright, as strong
As soldiers on parade.
Their scent carries through the air.
As the morning passes
The sun pounds down on the back of my neck,
And I seek the shade of the weeping willow tree.
I rest against the rough brown bark
Its rich green leaves cascading down.
I close my eyes and sit awhile,
Burnt in my mind -
The wonder
The beauty
Mother nature at its best.

Daniel Smith (12)
Westcliff High School for Boys

PIER 39, SAN FRANCISCO

Welcome to the theatre,
The stage in the sea.
Pier 39 had everything to entertain me.
As a backdrop on one side
Was Golden Gate Bridge,
Precisely painted with smoke effects swirling around,
Creating an eerie atmosphere.

On the other side was Alcatraz,
Imprisoning people's attention.
The set carefully positioned -
Toy shops, hat shops, clothes shops, joke shops,
Sweet shops packed with goodies galore.
The actors wearing costumes of trainers and shorts
Strolled from scene to scene.

The seals were the audience packed 20 to a seat.
They weren't the most fragrant guests
You could care to meet.
As the day came to an end,
The black velvet curtain of night fell.
Pier 39 is a place I remember well.

Luke Richardson (12)
Westcliff High School for Boys

HADLEIGH WOODS

As I entered the sun stricken woods,
I smelt a sweet smell coming from around me.
I went up to see what it was;
It was like sticky honey,
It was sap glistening in the sun.
I went on further,
Kicking the leaves, which rustled beneath my feet.
The path I was following diverted slightly to the right,
Where some of the trees were bare,
Stripped of their autumn clothes.
There was suddenly a colossal moss covered log in my way,
I stepped over it cautiously as I didn't want to slip,
A brightness caught my eye, with shades covering some up:
The sun was trying to creep through the giant brown and green canopy,
The sun went in and the woods became shady again.
Very quickly a creature darted in front of me.
At first I couldn't make out what it was;
It just looked like a brown fur ball,
But when I got closer I saw a timid fox,
Its eyes were deep red and fixed on me.
I was approaching the end of my walk.
There was a burning smell from my left;
I couldn't see any smoke, so I carried on.
I heard a slight rustling in a bush near to me,
A long snake was coiling around and around,
And I can remember running, running away from the woods.

James Laden (12)
Westcliff High School for Boys

FROM MY GRANDMOTHER'S BALCONY

As I look from the balcony,
Motley buildings meet my eyes:
One with pebble-dashed, whitewashed walls,
with chimneys sprouting up like plants,
thrusting their way to heaven.
A great brown block of flats covered in scaffold,
as simple as a brick, no style, no elegance.
Its green scaffold climbing up its walls
as if it were a vine that had taken hold.
Gazing below, down to the courtyard,
a small green patch, an oasis,
in the dull bleak desert of concrete.
Row upon row of garages,
all exactly the same.
Looking to my right, out to sea,
the mist and haze shields the far coast from my eyes:
The forbidding grey waters,
tossing boat and buoy aside.
Tired of the cold, I step inside,
and shut the door behind me.

Jonathan Lester (12)
Westcliff High School for Boys